Bullying

Other Books in the Current Controversies Series

Abortion

Animal Rights

College Admissions

Death Penalty

Drug Legalization

Gangs

Immigration

Medical Ethics

Military Families

Oil Spills

Pesticides

Racial Profiling

Same-Sex Marriage

Urban Sprawl

Vegetarianism

Violence in the Media

The Wage Gap

Bullying

Noah Berlatsky, Book Editor

GREENHAVEN PRESS
A part of Gale, Cengage Learning

GALE
CENGAGE Learning·

Farmington Hills, Mich • San Francisco • New York • Waterville, Maine
Meriden, Conn • Mason, Ohio • Chicago

Patricia Coryell, *Vice President & Publisher, New Products & GVRL*
Douglas Dentino, *Manager, New Products*
Judy Galens, *Acquisitions Editor*

For more information, contact:
Greenhaven Press
27500 Drake Rd.
Farmington Hills, MI 48331-3535
Or you can visit our Internet site at gale.cengage.com

Articles in Greenhaven Press anthologies are often edited for length to meet page requirements. In addition, original titles of these works are changed to clearly present the main thesis and to explicitly indicate the author's opinion. Every effort is made to ensure that Greenhaven Press accurately reflects the original intent of the authors. Every effort has been made to trace the owners of copyrighted material.

Cover image copyright © wavebreakmedia/Shutterstock.com.

LIBRARY OF CONGRESS CATALOGING-IN-PUBLICATION DATA

Bullying / Noah Berlatsky, book editor.
    pages cm. -- (Current controversies)
    Includes bibliographical references and index.
    ISBN 978-0-7377-7211-1 (hardcover) -- ISBN 978-0-7377-7212-8 (pbk.)
    1. Bullying. 2. Bullying in schools. 3. Cyberbullying. I. Berlatsky, Noah.
    BF637.B85B8432 2015
    302.34'3--dc23
                                                                2014040402

Printed in Mexico
1 2 3 4 5 6 7 19 18 17 16 15

Contents

Foreword   **15**

Introduction   **18**

Chapter 1: Is Bullying a Dangerous and Growing Problem?

Chapter Preface   **23**

**Yes: Bullying Is a Dangerous and
Growing Problem**

Bullying in Utah Is a Growing
and Dangerous Problem   **25**

Barbara Christiansen

Bullying is a serious problem for many school children
in Utah. Bullying can be done in person or online, and
the type and severity may vary from school to school or
case to case. Whatever the exact circumstances of bullying though, it can result in suicidal thoughts and missed
school days because students are afraid to go to school.
Schools and bystanders have a responsibility to intervene
to protect students and ensure that they can learn in
school without fear or anxiety.

The Effects of Bullying Last into Adulthood   **36**

Michelle Castillo

A study shows that bullying in school can have long-
term effects on victims. These effects include suicidal
thoughts into adulthood, difficulty forming adult social
relationships, and difficulties in keeping employment and
saving money. Bully-victims, students who both bullied
others and were bullied themselves, were the most likely
to have long-term consequences. Experts say that people
underestimate the emotional trauma and long-term effects of bullying.

Parents Should Be Held Liable
When Kids Bully   **40**

Jeremy Byellin

In some cases, when a student is bullied, parents may be able to seek damages from a school or school board. However, when a minor performs an illegal act, parents may also be held responsible. Parents probably would not have as much money as a school board, but if the goal is to deter bullying, suing the parents of the bully may be the most effective option.

No: Bullying Is Not a Dangerous and Growing Problem

Bullying Reports Are Increasing
but Not Bullying Itself
Anne Collier

43

Reporting on bullying has increased in the media. However, bullying itself has been consistently decreasing since the early 1990s. This includes decreases in both verbal harassment and physical violence. Bullying targeted at African American and Hispanic students has especially declined. The drop may be caused by increased psychiatric knowledge and better medicines. The prevalence of social media may also help, since it makes it easier to report problems and provides students with something to do besides engaging in criminal or bullying activities.

Bullying Does Not Cause Suicide

46

Deborah Temkin

Bullying can be one factor linked to suicide, but it does not cause suicide. Instead, many factors may cause teens to take their own lives, including mental health issues. Reporting that bullying is the cause of suicide is misleading and may be dangerous, since media reports of suicide can spur those at risk to attempt to take their own lives. Rather than saying that bullying causes suicide, schools, parents, and media need to recognize that both bullying and suicide are complex and serious problems, and work to address both.

Stop Panicking About Bullies

49

Nick Gillespie

Individual instances of bullying can be horrible, and people should work to reduce bullying. However, there is little evidence that bullying is worsening in the United States. Antibullying legislation has in fact mostly resulted in more paperwork and litigation, and has not clearly helped those who are bullied. Parents, teachers, and the media should recognize that childhood in the United States is much less violent and dangerous than in the past, and that bullying is a small, manageable problem, not a dangerous epidemic.

Chapter 2: Is Cyberbullying a Major Problem?

Chapter Preface   57

Yes: Cyberbullying Is a Major Problem

Cyberbullying Is Dangerous   59
Suzanne Phillips

Cyberbullying can be emotionally traumatic and painful. Students can be cyberbullied constantly; there is no escape when they leave school. In addition, cyberbullying may be more painful because it is so public; anyone with an Internet connection can see the abuse and read insults directed at the victim. To combat cyberbullying, parents and students need to document occurrences and be willing to speak to parents of bullies and school authorities, and possibly lawyers if the abuse does not stop.

Female Cyberbullying Is a Serious Problem   64
Lori O. Favela

Girls are especially prone to cyberbullying and to being cyberbullied. This is because girls are more likely to seek status through verbal attacks and exclusion, methods that are encouraged and abetted by the Internet. Cyberbullying among girls can have serious and painful consequences. Cyberbullying can be addressed through clear guidelines for Internet use in school and by teaching students to ignore cyberbullying and to engage courteously with each other online.

No: Cyberbullying Is Not a Major Problem

The Cyberbullying Problem Is Overhyped   70
Tim Cushing

Cyberbullying rates are frequently exaggerated by groups selling products that prevent or diminish the practice. For example, one-time incidents are classified as "bullying," even though bullying is usually understood as repeated harassment. Moreover, antibullying programs are generally ineffective, and some evidence suggests they may even make bullying worse. The exaggeration of cyberbullying may pull resources away from serious problems and result in a waste of time and money.

Cyberbullying Is Less Common than   76
Traditional Bullying
American Psychological Association
According to studies by psychologist Dan Olweus, traditional bullying remains substantially more prevalent than cyberbulling. Furthermore, when cyberbullying occurs, victims are generally also victims of traditional bullying. Cyberbullying can be a serious problem, but given the fact that traditional bullying is more prevalent, it is important to focus limited resources on that issue and treat cyberbullying as an important but secondary concern.

The Links Between Cyberbullying and   79
Suicide Are Oversimplified
Alison Auld
The media often claims that cyberbullying leads to teen suicide. This is an oversimplification; in fact, suicide is often linked to a range of factors, including mental health issues. Focusing on bullying alone can prevent parents and authorities from addressing the underlying mental health problems. Education on cyberbullying and on suicide is vital and needs to take place before antibullying legislation is passed. Journalists also need to do a better job explaining the complicated relationship between suicide and cyberbullying.

Cyberbullying Is Serious but Not   84
an Epidemic
Larry Magid

Though cyberbullying can be serious, it is not an epidemic. Cyberbullying has not been rising and the numbers are not that high. It is important not to overreport cyberbullying, because studies have shown that students are more likely to bully when they believe it is more common. It is also important to realize that all cyberbullying is not equally traumatic; in some instances, some students will handle cyberbullying themselves with no adverse effects.

Chapter 3: What Types of People Are Targeted for Bullying?

Chapter Preface   90

Bullied Boys: Why Bright Lads   92
Are Being Picked On
> The Independent
> Students, and especially boys, who do well in school are often singled out for bullying and abuse. Poorer students dislike being shown up, and they may retaliate against a good student with verbal or physical bullying. As a result, good students often deliberately do poorly in school to avoid attention from peers. Attention and awareness from parents and teachers can help stem the bullying, as can antibullying programs implemented in school.

LGBT Youth Suffer Long-Term Effects   96
from Bullying
> *J.A. Muraco and S.T. Russell*
> Lesbian, gay, bisexual, and transgender (LGBT) students often face serious bullying in school. So do students who are gender noncomforming—that is, students who are seen as having characteristics that are not normal for their gender. Research shows that bullying of LGBT and gender nonconforming students is related to long-term health problems, such as depression, as these young adults mature into adulthood. This demonstrates how serious bullying is and how important it is to confront bullying of LGBT and gender nonconforming students early on.

Muslim Youth in California Are Targeted   101
for Bullying
> *Council on American-Islamic Relations*

Though most Muslim students in California report good experiences in school, a significant number report being targeted for bullying. Bullying is related to ethnicity and religion. Girls who wear the *hijab*, or Muslim head scarf, may face especially severe bullying. Many Muslim parents do not know that they have options to deal with bullying and that discrimination on the basis of religion is illegal. Schools, teachers, and parents need to be aware that bullying of Muslim students is unacceptable.

Antibullying Campaigns Ignore Sexism   107
Against Girls and Women
  Meghan Murphy

Bullying programs in schools have grown in popularity. However, these programs ignore the problem of sexism and sexual harassment. Children learn from an early age that women can be targeted for violence and abuse; these lessons are brought into adulthood where sexual harassment remains a serious problem in numerous institutions, such as the Royal Canadian Mounted Police. There should be programs in schools specifically addressing the problems of sexism and sexual harassment, so as to protect girls as well as boys from bullying.

Despite Myths, Asian Americans Are   113
Not Disproportionately Bullied
  Nellie Tran

There is a common belief that Asian Americans are more bullied than other ethnic groups. This is not true; on the contrary, national studies have found that Asian Americans are the least bullied ethnic group overall. However, smaller studies have shown that some particular groups in specific situations—such as Asian American athletes—may experience high levels of bullying. Studies of bullying might do better to focus on subgroups of Asian Americans rather than looking at all Asian Americans as a single class.

Hispanic and Immigrant Students   117
Face Bullying
  José A. Healy

Latino immigrants are often the target of bullying because they don't fit in and are often relatively poor. Immigrants may especially be singled out in communities where there is not a tradition of immigration, so that new arrivals are seen as especially unusual or unwelcome. In many cases, Latinos from families that immigrated a generation or two ago will bully new immigrants. Communities need to make an effort to end bullying, and Latino communities in particular need to work together to empower both older and newer immigrants.

Chapter 4: How Does Bullying Affect Older Victims?

Chapter Preface   124

Cyberbullying Is a Problem in Universities   126
Vivian Luk

Cyberbullying and harassment is usually seen as a problem in middle or high schools. But new studies show it is prevalent in Canadian universities as well. Students report being harassed and targeted by peers, and even faculty report online harassment from students and colleagues. This harassment can result in emotional pain and even in suicidal thoughts. Universities need to formulate more specific policies to deal with cyberbullying and harassment.

Katherine Jenkins, Louise Mensch   130
and Lorraine Pascale Are Plagued by
Sexist Cyberbullies
Jojo Moyes

Women in the public eye or those who express their opinions online are often targeted for cyberbullying and abuse. This can include rape threats, death threats, and sustained harassment through social media or via e-mail. Some women ignore the bullying; others may confront it publicly. In either case, more laws are needed to deal with and prevent online harassment and bullying of women.

Workplace Bullying Is a Serious Problem   134
Catherine Mattice

Bullying occurs not just at school but in the workplace. Workers who are bullied may experience serious emotional distress and may even have suicidal thoughts. Workplace harassment may include aggressive communication, humiliation, and manipulation. People who are bullied at work should document each instance carefully in preparation for informing human resources or a lawyer. They may also want to start looking for a new job.

Teachers Face Bullying and   138
Hostile Workplaces
   Katie Osgood

Teachers face an extremely stressful, bullying work environment. They do not have the resources they need to teach students, they are asked to meet unrealistic goals, and they are regularly blamed and disrespected by administrators and politicians. The workplace conditions result in despair, exhaustion, and even in some cases in suicidal thoughts. Teachers need to fight back against the public condemnation and against the unfair abuse they receive.

NFL Bullies   144
   Emily Bazelon and Josh Levin

Bullying is an established part of National Football League (NFL) locker-room culture, with older players humiliating and playing pranks on younger ones, especially rookies. One of the worst cases has involved Richie Incognito of the Miami Dolphins, who has been repeatedly sanctioned for abusive behavior to fellow teammates, opponents, and officials. Allegations about Incognito's bullying of teammate Jonathan Martin were at first dismissed by the NFL, but as the revelations became more serious, the league was forced to take the matter more seriously and suspend Incognito. This may be a good first step toward creating a less abusive NFL culture.

Bullying Is a Problem in Police Academies   149
   David C. Couper

Many police departments use military-style training, in which instructors shout abusive language at and bully recruits. This is a poor way to train officers, since it shows them that abusive behavior of civilians is tolerated and even encouraged. It is also not a good method of imparting necessary information. Bullying and abuse have no place in the training of police officers, and their continued use in many police departments is troublesome.

Bullying Is a Problem in the Military   154
Margaret Carlson

A nineteen-year-old private, Danny Chen, committed suicide after hazing and bullying by his fellow soldiers in Afghanistan. This incident points to a systemic problem in the military, where individual soldiers are sometimes targeted for brutal hazing. The US Army is to be commended for admitting what happened to Chen and disciplining his abusers. However, more needs to be done to address the culture of bullying in the military.

Organizations to Contact   158

Bibliography   163

Index   168

Foreword

By definition, controversies are "discussions of questions in which opposing opinions clash" (*Webster's Twentieth Century Dictionary Unabridged*). Few would deny that controversies are a pervasive part of the human condition and exist on virtually every level of human enterprise. Controversies transpire between individuals and among groups, within nations and between nations. Controversies supply the grist necessary for progress by providing challenges and challengers to the status quo. They also create atmospheres where strife and warfare can flourish. A world without controversies would be a peaceful world; but it also would be, by and large, static and prosaic.

The Series' Purpose

The purpose of the Current Controversies series is to explore many of the social, political, and economic controversies dominating the national and international scenes today. Titles selected for inclusion in the series are highly focused and specific. For example, from the larger category of criminal justice, Current Controversies deals with specific topics such as police brutality, gun control, white collar crime, and others. The debates in Current Controversies also are presented in a useful, timeless fashion. Articles and book excerpts included in each title are selected if they contribute valuable, long-range ideas to the overall debate. And wherever possible, current information is enhanced with historical documents and other relevant materials. Thus, while individual titles are current in focus, every effort is made to ensure that they will not become quickly outdated. Books in the Current Controversies series will remain important resources for librarians, teachers, and students for many years.

In addition to keeping the titles focused and specific, great care is taken in the editorial format of each book in the series. Book introductions and chapter prefaces are offered to provide background material for readers. Chapters are organized around several key questions that are answered with diverse opinions representing all points on the political spectrum. Materials in each chapter include opinions in which authors clearly disagree as well as alternative opinions in which authors may agree on a broader issue but disagree on the possible solutions. In this way, the content of each volume in Current Controversies mirrors the mosaic of opinions encountered in society. Readers will quickly realize that there are many viable answers to these complex issues. By questioning each author's conclusions, students and casual readers can begin to develop the critical thinking skills so important to evaluating opinionated material.

Current Controversies is also ideal for controlled research. Each anthology in the series is composed of primary sources taken from a wide gamut of informational categories including periodicals, newspapers, books, US and foreign government documents, and the publications of private and public organizations. Readers will find factual support for reports, debates, and research papers covering all areas of important issues. In addition, an annotated table of contents, an index, a book and periodical bibliography, and a list of organizations to contact are included in each book to expedite further research.

Perhaps more than ever before in history, people are confronted with diverse and contradictory information. During the Persian Gulf War, for example, the public was not only treated to minute-to-minute coverage of the war, it was also inundated with critiques of the coverage and countless analyses of the factors motivating US involvement. Being able to sort through the plethora of opinions accompanying today's major issues, and to draw one's own conclusions, can be a complicated and frustrating struggle. It is the editors' hope that Current Controversies will help readers with this struggle.

Introduction

"Bullying in the 21st century has reached a whole new level. It involves the complex vortex of the internet."

In 2012, Amanda Todd became the face of bullying. Todd, a fifteen-year-old from Vancouver, Canada, committed suicide in October of that year after being bullied at multiple schools and struggling with depression. A video she made a month before, in which she used flashcards to describe the abuse and harassment she had endured, went viral after her death, receiving millions of views. Her story was covered in major news outlets and sparked a growing debate about bullying and online harassment.

In her video, Todd explains that in seventh grade she and friends had used webcams to chat with strangers. In one of these chats, the older man she was talking to convinced her to flash her breasts. A year later, the man contacted her and threatened to release the image of her topless if she didn't pose for more nude images. She refused, and he publicized the image widely, sending it to friends, family members, and classmates.

Even after she switched schools, the image followed her, as the man continued posting it on social media. She struggled with depression and anxiety and was targeted repeatedly for bullying by classmates who called her "porn star" and worse. After being beaten up by a group of girls, she attempted suicide, but was rescued. The bullying and depression continued, however, and she eventually succeeded at taking her life.

Much of the discussion surrounding Todd's death focused on bullying and cyberbullying. The United Kingdom-based *Daily Mirror*, for example, ran a story under the headline

"Suicide Girl's Mum Reveals More Harrowing Details of Cyber Bullying Campaign That Drove Her Daughter to Her Death," and *Jezebel* later ran one titled "Arrest Made in Connection to Amanda Todd Cyber Bullying Case." Sarah Fader, at the blog site *amotherworld*, said that Todd's story showed that "bullying in the 21st century has reached a whole new level. It involves the complex vortex of the internet."[1] Fader added,

> When I was in junior high school, I was severely bullied. I woke up every day terrified to go to school. My heart palpitated uncontrollably at the thought that I would have to see those two girls (who I was once friends with) that now made every day in 8th grade a living hell. I'm still traumatized when I think about what I went through.
>
> But I survived; Amanda Todd did not.[2]

For Fader, then, the bullying of Todd is an extension of the bullying Fader herself was subjected to at school.

Emily Bazelon at *Slate*, however, argues that seeing Todd's story solely through the lens of bullying may be deceptive. Bazelon points out that Todd's struggles began, not with teasing by peers, but with an older man who singled her out and stalked her. Bazelon writes:

> Why don't the headlines about Amanda Todd say "Stalked Teen Commits Suicide" rather than "Bullied Teen"? This isn't about semantics: It's about understanding what appears to have propelled this girl on a terrible downward spiral, which, based on what we know, included drug and alcohol abuse. Clearly she was vulnerable to depression, the major

---

1. Sarah Fader, "Cyber Bullying Should Be Stopped: Amanda Todd Story," *amotherworld*, October 15, 2012. http://amotherworld.com/main/parenting/cyber-bullying-must-be-stopped-amanda-todd-story.

2. Ibid.

trigger for suicide—substance abuse is also a risk factor—and that's another part of the story that's not getting enough attention.[3]

Bazelon adds that in this case, "the real victimizer was a creepy scary adult, not a teen bully, and that whatever happened in school was secondary to the damage that adult did."[4]

If the issue is stalking rather than bullying, then the social and legal response should also be somewhat different. Certainly, kids need to be taught that bullying is damaging and unacceptable. But even more they need to learn to be careful of strangers, and especially adult strangers, online and to protect their privacy. Legal remedies should focus less on criminalizing bullying and more on tracking down online adult predators.

In 2014, Canadian police arrested a twenty-five-year-old Dutch citizen suspected to be the man who took Todd's picture. He was charged with, among other things, extortion and possession and distribution of child pornography. In addition to blackmailing Todd, he is supposed to have targeted numerous other minors as well as older male victims in Europe, Britain, and Canada. The arrest, again, suggests that Todd's story was not only, or even primarily, about bullying, but was instead the result of the actions of an adult criminal, who deliberately abused not just Todd but many others.

The rest of *Current Controversies: Bullying* focuses on other issues surrounding bullying in such chapters as: "Is Bullying a Dangerous and Growing Problem?," "Is Cyberbullying a Major Problem?," "What Types of People Are Targeted for Bullying?," and "How Does Bullying Affect Older Victims?" Throughout,

---

3. Emily Bazelon, "Amanda Todd Was Stalked Before She Was Bullied," *Slate*, October 18, 2012. www.slate.com/blogs/xx_factor/2012/10/18/suicide_victim_amanda_todd _stalked_before_she_was_bullied.html.

4. Ibid.

writers present different viewpoints on whether bullying is dangerous, how dangerous it is, who it affects, and what can be done to stop it.

CHAPTER 1

Is Bullying a Dangerous and Growing Problem?

Chapter Preface

When people talk about bullying, they usually focus on children targeting or harassing their peers. However, children are not the only ones who bully. In some cases, parents may harass and bully their own children.

Prin Dumas at NJ.com argues that bullying by parents that stops short of actual physical or sexual abuse is often ignored or downplayed. But, she says, "If bullying in schools is harmful, isn't bullying at home worse?" She adds, "Threats, rumors, physical and verbal abuse, and emotional and mental manipulation are all actions at the disposal of a parent. Sadly, I believe we could all think of a parent bully off the top of our heads."[1]

Nancy S. Buck at *Psychology Today* points to some extreme examples of parental abuse and bullying, including Jessica Beagley of Alaska, who was convicted of child abuse for punishing her seven-year-old by spreading hot sauce on him and giving him cold showers, and Julie Schenecker of Tampa, Florida, who killed her teenaged son and daughter when they talked back to her.

Buck notes that Beagley and Schenecker are unusual, but she sees them as indicative of a particular philosophy of parenting in which "people believe that children need to be controlled."[2] Buck says that this approach to parenting leads to bribing, grounding, and other "disconnecting, bullying approaches" to controlling children.

1. Prin Dumas, "Bullying in Children: When Parents Are the Bully," NJ.com, June 14, 2013. www.nj.com/parenting/index.ssf/2013/06/bullying_in_children_when_parents_are_the_bully.html.

2. Nancy S. Buck, "Calling All Parents: Stop Bullying, Start Teaching," *Psychology Today*, March 10, 2011. www.psychologytoday.com/blog/peaceful-parenting/201103/calling-all-parents-stop-bullying-start-teaching.

Instead, Buck says, parents need to work with their children. "A parent is not responsible for *controlling* his child," she argues. "A parent is responsible for *teaching* her child how to control her own behavior. Let's stop trying to control and change children's behavior. Let's stop bullying and abusing our children."[3]

Ronit Baras, writing at the blog site *Family Matters*, suggests that when parents bully, it is not because of a flawed parenting philosophy but rather because they experienced violence and abuse themselves. "Parents bully their kids because they have been bullied themselves as children or they are being bullied by someone else," she says. "Often, people who have been bullied as children do not realize that their behavior is bullying."[4] Baras discusses a range of possible bullying behavior by parents, including physical abuse such as hitting or denying a child food, and emotional abuse, such as threatening the child, name calling, humiliating the child in public, or being overly controlling. She notes that such abuse can have life-long health consequences for children.

The remainder of this chapter looks at other issues of bullying and the dangers of bullying, including questions about how dangerous bullying is and whether it is increasing or decreasing.

3. Ibid.

4. Ronit Baras, "Bullying (23): Bully Parents," *Family Matters*, April 4, 2011. www.ronitbaras.com/emotional-intelligence/personal-development-c/bullying-23 -bully-parents.

Bullying in Utah Is a Growing and Dangerous Problem

Barbara Christiansen

Barbara Christiansen covers American news for the Daily Herald, *the daily newspaper for Provo, Utah.*

When Jim was a third-grader, he was half nerd and half athlete.

Suicidal Thoughts

"Neither group would really accept me," he said. "They didn't really understand how I worked. It got to the point where there were a lot of degrading comments. People would throw stuff at me if I tried to get on the playground."

He knew what the kids were calling him. He also knew one way to make it stop.

"I had a large vocabulary. I knew what suicide was. I almost got to that point. No one knew. I didn't tell anybody."

Jim, a Karl G. Maeser Preparatory Academy student who asked that his real name not be used, is not alone in feeling left out, teased and bullied by his peers. The National Education Association reports that six of 10 American teenagers witness bullying in school every day. An estimated 160,000 students stay home each day out of fear of being bullied. About 71 percent of students report bullying as an ongoing problem.

Utah students are not immune.

In Utah, 23.2 percent of males ages 10–18 say suicidal thoughts are because of problems at school, and 57.7 percent of females ages 10–18 say suicide attempts are caused by problems with relationships, according to the Utah Department of

Health. And in a survey of Utah's parents from the Human Rights Education Center of Utah, three-fourths of parents had concerns with bullying, bias and problems in the home, school or community because of a lack of diversity education, training or awareness.

As common as bullying is, statistics show that no action is taken in about 85 percent of bullying cases; either the incidents are not reported or the schools do nothing.

Bullying is more than teasing, making jokes or "boys being boys." It's more than throwing punches or pushing a child down. It can include name-calling, calling a student gay or a girl a slut, spreading rumors or mocking a person's differences, either in person, behind a child's back or through the Internet or cell phones. It can be pushing a peer around or physically harming him. The less powerful are frequently targeted.

Bullying does more than make life unpleasant for the picked-on students. It can damage their self-esteem, cause depression, distract them from school, hurt academic performance and cause them to be afraid to go to school. In some cases the effects reach into adulthood or worse, to death. Research has indicated that bullying victims are more likely to attempt or complete suicide than their peers who are not bullied.

And yet, as common as bullying is, statistics show that no action is taken in about 85 percent of bullying cases; either the incidents are not reported or the schools do nothing.

The difficulty comes first in defining bullying, then in recognizing it in schools, church groups, playgrounds and neighborhoods. Putting an end to bullying also is not an easy task, because it requires more than just teachers and administrators catching and punishing bullies. It also requires parents to recognize it, empowering victims to come forward and teaching children to be the one who confronts the bully.

It's no easy task, but Utah County schools are taking it on.

"A person being bullied needs to know that we care about them and would hope that they would tell their parents or their teacher," said Greg Hudnall, the associate superintendent of the Provo School District and the administrator the police call when a student has committed suicide. "While I appreciate the concern that we may be focusing too much on bullying, my only response to that is, ask that to the child who is being bullied."

Ever since I came to this school it has been nothing but bullying. I have been bullied my whole life, from kindergarten through sixth grade.

Not So Happy Valley

Tatum Berthold, now a student at Maeser Preparatory Academy, was bullied at her last school.

"I was bullied for most of my elementary school experience," she said. "I remember my siblings talking about that junior high is the worst. It happened in elementary school when I was not ready.

"I would walk around—we had a big track—all along whistling songs of my sadness. I didn't have any friends. People called me teacher's pet. My teachers were the only friends I had in the world. That is why I am better around adults. I have ADHD. I wasn't medicated at that time. Just stupid things happened to me."

"I was in a play, 'Treasure Island,'" she said. "One of my lines was to insult someone." For that she used a word that some of the students didn't know, and they asked her what it meant. "I told them the definition of that word. They ended up calling me that and finding different ways to use it."

Maeser student Mahron Howard found herself on the receiving end of a hurtful wordplay on her name.

"I was called 'moron' all the time," she said. She was reluctant to ask for help. "It is not one of those things you go to your parents. You don't want them to fix it. You want the kids to fix it. I didn't really have any friends until about fourth grade."

The group of students from Maeser are part of a student advocate program, selected by the teachers and staff to help reduce bullying incidents. Many are in the group because they've felt the effects of being bullied. This group invited the *Daily Herald* to sit in on a meeting and hear their stories.

Sixth-grader Emma Graff from Provo's Spring Creek Elementary School calls herself a snitch. Others have resented that and bullied her.

"A girl said I was hateful, and that nobody likes me 'cause I am bossy," she said. "She was mad at me because there was fighting here at school. Ever since I came to this school it has been nothing but bullying. I have been bullied my whole life, from kindergarten through sixth grade." She transferred to her new school at the beginning of sixth grade.

"For me it wasn't only like being bullied, but my friends being bullied," Sara Lynsky from Karl G. Maeser Preparatory Academy said. "It was hard. When I was little it wasn't at school. People picked on me at swim team—the kids and the coaches. People told me I wouldn't ever be a great swimmer and it hurt."

"At my last meet one of the swim coaches—I went up to her and admitted that wasn't my best," she said.

"That is because you are doing crappy in practice," Sara remembers the coach saying.

Sara was suffering from tendinitis, but the coach told her to work through it. "I don't care how much that hurts," Sara recalled the coach saying to her. "You need to keep pushing yourself."

"She didn't tell me how I could improve," Sara said.

Dominic Greco, a third-grader, has also been pushed around.

"I was outside and a kid came up to me when I was on a swing," he said. "He pushed me off and he got on. He was about in the fourth or fifth grade. It just made me feel mad. After, he called me a word. I didn't know what the word meant, but it was like when someone calls you stupid."

The Factor of Fear

Provo School District sent home a survey this spring to gauge parents' and students' thoughts on bullying in the district. Of the respondents, 2.8 percent of secondary school students skipped school in the past month for fear that someone would physically hurt them and 6.3 percent would do the same, fearing they would be hurt emotionally or socially.

On the elementary school level, 12.9 percent feared being harassed, bothered or made fun of by a student. 6.1 percent feared being physically hurt. Being excluded from activities was a concern for 9.2 percent of the students.

More than one in 10 students felt they were the subject of rumors or gossip.

Tracking bullying is getting harder because of the advent of technology.

Secondary students faced some similar concerns. Of those who responded, 7.5 percent reported they were made fun of because of their size, and 3 percent were left out of because of race or culture, with 3.2 percent left out because of religion.

Seven percent felt they had been the target of rumors or gossip and 6.8 percent had been verbally harassed or made fun of.

"While our research may be smaller than anticipated because not as many parents or students took the survey, we are seeing more aggression from the bullies than in the past," Hudnall said. "Regardless, any act of bullying is inappropriate and will not be tolerated."

However, tracking bullying is getting harder because of the advent of technology. Doran Williams, the associate director of Wasatch Mental Health in Provo, said they do not keep statistics about how many bullying cases happen, but based on his experience cell phones have resulted in an increase in bullying.

"The reason for that is the ability to bully," he said. "Twenty-five years ago they didn't have cyberbullying. Kids didn't have cell phones. Technology gives an anonymous way to do it. I think there is more means to do it."

"The majority of kids in junior high and up have cell phones," he said. "They can take a picture and can post things instantaneously."

What Bullying Looks Like

Facebook posts, cell phone pictures and cyberstalking have joined the ranks of fighting, name-calling and gossiping as acts of bullying.

"The research definition of bullying shows three important things—the intent to harm, a high frequency of the problem or behavior and a power differential," Scott Ross, an assistant professor at Utah State University and a specialist in behavior support systems, said. "The bully must be more powerful than the victim," he said.

Defining bullying is the easy part. Recognizing those factors on the playground is a much different story.

"Imagine you are an adult on the playground or school," he said. "It's hard to figure out whether there is an intent to hurt or a power differential. That's really difficult for adults to do. That's why there is such a low frequency of reporting. For the kids it's even harder. It becomes an arbitrary line."

Bullying takes different forms depending on geography.

"You'll see more cyberbullying in higher socioeconomic status areas," Ross said. "In Tennessee, there is a big bullying behavior, with kids coming back with a bigger insult, and going back and forth, often resulting in fights. In California, it was actually more around saying things like 'you're stupid.' Depending on the culture of the school you're going to see bullying look different."

Bullying can take many forms, including physical, verbal, emotional or cyberbullying. Kids can be punched, pushed, shoved or otherwise intimidated to provide a feeling of power or superiority for the bully. They may be called names or have embarrassing information shared about them. Cyberbullying—using technology to harm another—is relatively new. It often is done through means that do not reveal the instigator. That doesn't make it less hurtful.

It is hard to protect kids when we don't know who the opposition is.

Brian Drake, a seventh-grader at American Fork Junior High School, has been on the receiving end of a mocking Facebook post.

"A girl in my band class posted that I looked like a retarded mushroom from Mario," he said. "A lot of people saw it and they started saying it to me at school."

Syd Hackford, assistant principal of Lone Peak High School, said cyberbullying is increasing.

"It's a new style of bullying that allows the bully to be anonymous," she said. "It is hard to protect kids when we don't know who the opposition is."

That anonymity can contribute to the bullying escalating quickly. Recent threats to one teenager at the school required law enforcement intervention.

"A girl had no idea who was sending threatening text messages," Hackford said. "She came to me for help. She emailed copies of the conversations. I confirmed they are absolutely harassing."

The person who sent the messages used an app to disguise his or her identity.

"Are they in this classroom? Do I see them at lunch?" Hackford said the victim is wondering. "We have an obligation to offer support and help the person through a difficult situation," Hackford said. "She is thinking about this and it is keeping her from giving her full attention to school."

"The toughest ones to deal with are kids who are fearful to be at school because they don't know who is bullying them," she said. "It is coming through digital devices through anonymous sources. We need to put the focus back on our primary function, which is learning. Kids get quite traumatized by these incidents."

Longterm Effects

Joshua Jones has children of his own, but he still sometimes thinks about being a child in his neighborhood who didn't go to church with the rest of the kids.

"My father was not LDS [Church of Latter Day Saints, or Mormons] and my mother was LDS, but an inactive member," Jones, an Orem resident, said. "I grew up with kids who were LDS and they would often torment me and pick on me for not going to church. I tried very hard to be friends with these kids, but there was no hope. They would ignore me at lunch and sometimes even trip me and play mean pranks on me.

"One occasion that stands out was when one of the kids invited me to his birthday party. I was so excited. I thought maybe people were starting to come around. I told him the day before his party that I was excited and he told me he only invited me because his mom made him, and he would be very embarrassed if I were to come because I didn't go to church."

I had one mom say that she didn't like me coming over to her house because I was scuzzy.

"I had his present already," he said. "I went home and was looking at it, crying. My mom came home and saw me crying. I told her I was not really invited because he was embarrassed because I don't go to church. My mom said I could keep the present and she and I would go out and do something nice."

That wasn't the only time his parents stood behind him. Sometimes too they stood up for him, when his tormentors were a little bigger than he was.

"It was not only the kids, I found out," Jones said. "Their parents a lot of times were just as cruel. I had one mom say that she didn't like me coming over to her house because I was scuzzy. I went riding on my bike past another house and the dad chased me down and rubbed car wax in my hair.

"His son was a big jock and I was scrawny," he said. "My dad was a big man. He scared the living hell out of that man. The man told him he was just joking, but my dad pointed out that I was crying. 'He wasn't having fun, and you are an adult.'"

Yet turning to his parents sometimes made his situation worse; kids, he knew, are supposed to play with other kids.

"It isolated me even more," Jones said. "I felt very alone a lot of times."

"All of this started because I didn't go to church," he said. "The good kids who should have been encouraging me to go to church with them terrified me of going to church. I tried to be nice to everyone regardless of what they did to me. The behavior from these kids gave me many sad and lonely moments."

He said he is affected still.

"To this day I will bump into them," he said. "They tell me that I was always so nice to them. They didn't try to prove anything to me anymore, but they did some really mean things to me."

"It still sticks with me a little bit," he said. "I am not quite happy with how I was treated. I think about it every day. There are aspects where I catch myself maybe feeling sorry for myself. I always worry that I am saying and doing the right thing so nobody has any ability to say anything about what I say or do. I am very conscious about it. I worry sometimes more about what people think based on what happened, but for the most part I do what I can and have just moved past it. Sometimes it is not easy."

Bystanders possess a great deal of power to shift attention away from the negative and toward the positive.

The Bystander Effect

Bullies like an audience.

Professor Ross said bullies tend to act in groups or to act in front of a group of bystanders. They like the attention. Almost nine out of 10 bullying incidents happen while a bystander is watching and laughing, which encourages the bully to keep bullying.

But groups can work in favor of the victim as well.

"At the beginning of the year I had a ninth-grader come up, grab me by the throat and pin me to the wall," Brian Drake, who was also cyberbullied by a bandmate, said. "His friend shoved me. It really hurt. They did it because they thought it was funny. They both walked away laughing about it. It was right outside the principal's office, too."

So Brian tipped the numbers in his favor.

"A bunch of friends who were ninth-graders said they would protect me," he said.

That's exactly what Ross and his organization, the Stand for Courage Foundation, are encouraging.

"Bystanders possess a great deal of power to shift attention away from the negative and toward the positive," the group's website says.

Since at least some of the motivation seems to come from gaining attention, the organization is working to remove that attention and shift it to those who are responding correctly to discourage bullying.

"We are working to catch the kids in the school doing right," Ross said. "We are reinforcing them for responding the right way."

And it makes a difference. Tatum Berthold, who was teased using a word she'd explained to her tormentors, found an unexpected hero one day.

"There was a pack of bullies, guys who were jocks," Tatum said. "They would always bully weaklings, underdogs. One was in my ward. I would have to go to church with him. He was a bystander." She said when the others called her the name they got from the lines of the play she was in, he stood up for her.

"I didn't want to be called that. The bystander in my neighborhood stood up from picking up some of his things. He looked at his pack of friends and looked at me. He said, 'Don't call her that. She is not that.' Almost everybody turned and looked at him and their jaws dropped. Ever since then I have had large respect for him."

The boy did not lose his friends because he stood up for her.

"His pack of friends kept him in that pack," she said. "They have said they realized and respect him enough for the bravery. In a million years I will never forget that. That was one of the reasons that gave me hope. I am someone people can care about. It will always make me respect him forever."

The Effects of Bullying Last into Adulthood

Michelle Castillo

Michelle Castillo is an associate editor for CBSNews.com.

Being bullied as a child may have long-lasting repercussions that can follow into adulthood.

A Lifelong Problem

A new study published in *Psychological Science* on Aug. 19 [2013] shows that being bullied as a youth was linked to more struggles to hold a regular job, more health problems and poor social relationships when the victim became an adult.

"We cannot continue to dismiss bullying as a harmless, almost inevitable, part of growing up," Dieter Wolke, a professor in the department of psychology at the University of Warwick in the U.K. [United Kingdom], said in a press release. "We need to change this mindset and acknowledge this as a serious problem for both the individual and the country as a whole; the effects are long-lasting and significant."

About 20 percent of U.S. students in grades 9 through 12 were bullied at some point in 2011, according to a Centers for Disease Control and Prevention survey.

For the new study, researchers looked at 1,420 children between the ages of nine to 16, and followed up with them when they were 24 through 26 years old. Each participant was surveyed four to six times during the study.

Researchers were particularly interested in the impact on victims, bullies and people who were in both categories, which they called "bully-victims."

All three groups were twice as likely to have problems with maintaining employment and actively saving money when they grew up compared to those who weren't involved in bullying. They were also all more likely to have financial problems as adults.

[Bully-victims] were more than six times more likely to have a serious illness, smoke regularly or develop a psychiatric disorder compared to those who did not bully anyone at all.

In addition, the subjects had problems forming adult social relationships, meaning it was hard for them to have long-term friendships or good relationships with their parents. This was the same whether or not the person was married.

But when all factors were considered, just being a bully was shown to have very little impact on adult problems. Kids who bullied were more likely to have childhood psychiatric problems and difficulties with their family, which may have accounted for their problems later in life.

The people who may have been worst off were the bully-victims. They had the greatest chance of developing health problems as an adult: They were more than six times more likely to have a serious illness, smoke regularly or develop a psychiatric disorder compared to those who did not bully anyone at all.

"In the case of bully-victims, it shows how bullying can spread when left untreated," Wolke added. "Some interventions are already available in schools but new tools are needed to help health professionals to identify, monitor, and deal with the ill-effects of bullying. The challenge we face now is committing the time and resources to these interventions to try and put an end to bullying."

Previous studies had linked being bullied to increased risk of adult psychiatric problems. Teens bullied by their peers are

2.5 times more likely to have suicidal thoughts than those who haven't been recently bullied, an October 2012 study in the *Archives of Pediatric Medicine* showed.

Emotional Trauma

Emma-Jane Cross, founder of the anti-bullying charity Beat-Bullying, added that the study shows that bullying can affect society and the economy.

"The findings demonstrate for the first time just how far-reaching and damaging the consequences of bullying can be," she told the BBC.

It's more than just monetary and social consequences at risk. Psychologist Guy Winch told *TIME* that emotional trauma might be as harmful as physical injuries. One particular study using brain image scans showed that people who have been rejected have the same areas of the brain activated as those who are experiencing physical pain, he said.

"The intensity of the emotional pain bullying elicits, and the fact that other people underestimate how much hurt they feel makes being bullied an incredibly traumatic experience that can leave significant emotional scars," says Winch, who wrote *Emotional First Aid: Practical Strategies for Treating Failure, Rejection, Guilt, and Other Everyday Psychological Injuries.*

The bullies don't have to be the child's classmates. A June [2013] study in *Pediatrics* showed that people who were bullied by their siblings may have more adult mental health problems like depression and anxiety than those who had been bullied by their peers.

Winch said that targeting certain issues that affect bullied victims may be able to help prevent any further damage. Areas of focus should include building up their self-esteem, helping them heal from the emotional pain, helping them manage their anger and aggression and aiding them in understanding that they are wanted and belong.

"Some people are more resilient and tend to do some of these healing and curative things naturally. They might seek out their close friends and get emotional support from them, and by doing so remind themselves that they're accepted and appreciated," Winch said.

Parents Should Be Held Liable When Kids Bully

Jeremy Byellin

Jeremy Byellin is a Minneapolis attorney practicing in the areas of family law and estate planning.

Bullying in schools has become an increasingly serious problem.

The perpetrators of the 1999 Columbine High School massacre were discovered to have previously been the victims of bullying.

Several subsequent school shooting perpetrators were likewise the victims of bullying.

Notwithstanding its role in school shootings, bullying is also directly linked to teen suicides—and at a much higher incidence rate.

Liability

Is anyone legally liable when these tragedies occur?

According to Jill and Jim Moore, the parents of the late Alex Moore, the county board of education in which this bullying occurred is liable.

Alex was the victim of bullying at her high school, and tragically took her own life in May of 2010 at the age of 15.

The Moores filed suit in May of 2012 against the Chilton County Alabama Board of Education, claiming that the board both violated Alex's constitutional right to bodily integrity . . . and discriminated against her because of her disability (under the Rehabilitation Act and the Americans with Disabilities Act [ADA]).

These violations, according to the complaint, led to Alex's untimely death.

The complaint lists a brief recent history of bullying in the U.S. along with several actions taken by the federal government directing schools on steps to take to minimize bullying on school grounds.

According to the complaint, this is proof that the school should have been on notice to take action about bullying.

Alex "was often singled out by the senior boys, to the perverse delight of onlookers, including the bus driver employed by the school."

This bullying, described in the complaint, details some truly cruel and shocking acts against Alex, who was targeted because she was "overweight" and suffered from Blount's disease, a growth disorder that causes the lower leg to angle inward (making the person appear bow-legged).

For instance, Alex was regularly "the target of 'pig races' on the school bus."

The object of this game was "for senior boys to chase and catch a girl that they thought was the ugliest and fattest girl, and to kiss that girl on the cheek."

Alex "was often singled out by the senior boys, to the perverse delight of onlookers, including the bus driver employed by the school."

Parental Responsibility

The complaint alleges that school officials were aware of this activity, but remained indifferent (or, in the case of this school bus driver, implicitly encouraged it).

Nevertheless, the complaint ventures into uncharted territory, at least to a small extent.

Official school policy seemingly condemns bullying, in contrast to some previous lawsuits, so the plaintiffs have to show either that the school board either failed to properly train or supervise its employees; or had a widespread "custom" detached from its policies that condoned bullying.

On top of that, the plaintiffs will have to show that either of these caused the bullying to some significant degree.

Neither of these showings is impossible, nor are they easy in any sense.

If the lawsuit fails, who's responsible for the behavior of the bullying minors?

Surprising as this may come to some, their parents.

Legally speaking, minors above a certain age are liable for their own tortious actions, but effectively, their parents are the ones who end up taking the fall for them in court.

Considering the outrageousness of some of this bullying, I would be surprised if these minors were able to escape tort liability.

Of course, individual students are not as big of a target for lawsuits as deeper-pocketed school boards.

However, if such lawsuits are to be viewed as mechanisms to deter bullying, it's much more effective to target individuals instead of the school board itself.

Nonetheless, though deterrence may now be of very little help to Jim and Jill Moore, it may very well be motivating them to help prevent future tragedies such as the case of Alex Moore.

Bullying Reports Are Increasing but Not Bullying Itself

Anne Collier

Anne Collier is editor of NetFamilyNews.org and founder and executive director of its parent organization, Net Family News, Inc. She codirects ConnectSafely.org, a web-based resource for parents, educators, and others interested in the impact of the fixed and mobile social web on youth.

Do people ever consider the possibility that, if they're exposed to increased reports about a social problem, it's the reporting that has increased rather than the problem? It's increasingly clear that this is the case with school bullying: Only news reports about it have increased, not the behavior itself. In fact, both bullying and fear of it are down among US middle school students (the grade levels that tends to experience bullying most), *Education Week* reports, citing new numbers from the National Center for Educational Statistics.

This is data reflecting both physical and verbal aggression. For all students in grades 6–12, "hate-related graffiti" in school classrooms, bathrooms, hallways, etc. "dropped from about 36% in 1999 to about 28% in 2011. The rate of students who reported fearing an attack or harm at school at all has also dropped dramatically, from nearly 12% in 1995 to less than 4% in 2011. For black and Hispanic students, it's an even more encouraging shift—from more than 20% of both groups of students worried about being attacked at school to less than 5% in 2011 [the latest figures available]."

Large Decline in School Violence

The decline in actual physical violence in schools is even more dramatic: It was down 74% between 1992 and 2010, according to the latest US Department of Justice data, which was cited by David Finkelhor, director of the Crimes Against Children Research Center at the University of New Hampshire, in a paper he published last January.

Bullying is a problem but not a growing one, and far from the epidemic it's sometimes reported to be in the news media.

"The surveys that reflect change over the longest time periods, going back to the early 1990s, consistently show declines in bullying and peer victimization, some of it remarkably large. The more recent trends, since 2007, show some declines, but less consistently." This is true internationally too. Dr. Finkelhor cited a study of bullying in the journal *Social Psychology of Education* showing a decrease in bullying in all nine data sets the authors reviewed.

What about cyberbullying? Online harassment increased from 6% in 2000 to 9% in 2005 to 11% in 2010, and it's interesting to note that it increased less between 2005 and '10 than in the first 5 years tracked. Because social media is very much a reflection of school social life for young people, the peer aggression seen in social media is a lot like the peer aggression seen on school bathroom walls. So once it finds its "dead level," it will probably decline in the same way verbal and written aggression have.

So why do we so often default to worst-case scenarios where young people are concerned? Bullying is a problem but not a growing one, and far from the epidemic it's sometimes reported to be in the news media. And there are other positive social indicators: both homicide and suicide rates are down among young people, Finkelhor reported.

Possible Explanations

Besides consumer education and crime prevention at the societal level, he offers two other possible explanations for this downward trend in victimization of self and others:

1. Psychiatric medications and better access to mental healthcare

2. Digital media and communications on phones and the Web.

The rise of social media is another thing people don't typically think of as a positive force in society. But consider this point from Finkelhor: "These technologies may have dampened crime and bullying by providing more ways of summoning help, more forms of social surveillance, and engrossing activities that undermine forms of alienation that lead to crime." . . .

None of which is to say the problem has been solved. Parts of it—e.g., harassment and bullying of LGBT [lesbian, gay, bisexual, and transgender] youth and students with special needs—still need a great deal of attention and effort. But over all, Finkelhor wrote, "advocates and young people should feel inspired. Change can happen and it can get better." And I propose that, if we adults can collectively show greater acceptance that most young people are kind and respectful toward each other most of the time they will respond positively to that confidence and respect in them.

Bullying Does Not Cause Suicide

Deborah Temkin

Deborah Temkin is the bullying prevention manager at the Robert F. Kennedy Center for Justice and Human Rights.

Like many, I was saddened to read the latest headlines about two girls—one from Florida and one from Louisiana—who died by suicide earlier this month [September 2013]. While their families, friends, and communities grieve, the battle cry has started once again—"we must stop bullying because that's what caused these young girls' deaths." When headlines were made in September 2010 with a string of five young men who died by suicide seemingly because of bullying, the latest era of bullying prevention and anti-bullying campaigns was launched around this very fear—bullying causes suicide so we must prevent bullying. But there's a problem. The more we insist that bullying is the "cause" behind these suicides, the more we lose sight of the other factors that also likely played a role; and the more we insist that suicide is the "normal" outcome of bullying, the more we may actually be driving kids to that very idea.

Only One Factor

Don't get me wrong, of course we know that bullying is a factor in youth suicide. One study by researchers at Yale University estimated the risk of suicidal ideation was between two to nine times higher for youth who were bullied. It is not just those bullied at risk; in fact, several emerging studies suggest that those who both are bullied and bully others are at the highest risk for suicidality, and those who witness bullying are also at risk. But risk is not the same as cause. The vast majority of the estimated 28 percent of youth between the ages of 12 to 18 who report being bullied (9 percent report being cyberbullied) will not think about or engage in suicidal behaviors. In addition, only a small percentage of reported youth suicides specifically listed bullying as a precipitating factor (around 3.2 percent from 2005–2008).

We need to recognize that bullying prevention alone will not prevent suicide.

We cannot prevent suicide by simply preventing bullying, and we should not simply prevent bullying for fear of suicide. Yet, the ever present "youth commits suicide because of bullying" headlines seem to suggest as much. Let's consider the particular case from Florida that recently made headlines. Though very apparent that the young girl was targeted through cellphone-based social media, it has also been reported she was hospitalized for mental health and switched schools. It is not clear whether mental health services or other support continued after the youth left the hospital and attended the new school. We also don't know anything else that was potentially happening elsewhere in the youth's life. We simply do not know the whole story to be able to say that bullying was the sole cause.

Media Coverage May Also Be a Factor

We also have to consider that perhaps the recent media attention to such suicides is itself a risk factor for these youth. Phoebe Prince. Tyler Clementi. Jaime Rodemeyer. And the list goes on. These are all youth whose names, if not for their deaths and the reported bullying they faced, we would never know. With every additional media report of another youth dying by suicide "because of" bullying we reinforce the notion to at-risk youth that suicide is a normal reaction to bullying, and not only that, these media reports suggest that if they do die by suicide, their name will be known across the country and perhaps the world—something any youth who feels alone and invisible could desire. Suicide contagion has long been known to be a risk with certain types of reporting, with the strongest effect on adolescents. If we continue to report on youth suicide in this manner we may truly be exacerbating the very thing we want to prevent.

So what can we do? First, we need to recognize that bullying is a problem whether or not it leads to suicide, and we must take active steps to prevent it and provide support to those who feel they have been bullied. In parallel, we need to recognize that bullying prevention alone will not prevent suicide. Schools and parents need to understand the warning signs and prevention for both. Second, we must recognize the other factors that contribute, often alongside bullying, to a youth's decision to die by suicide. We must follow best practices for reporting on suicide—refraining from describing the means by which the youth died and avoiding quoting first responders and parents about the cause of the suicide. We must stop sensationalizing every youth who has died by suicide, remembering that such reporting could be the very catalyst for the next youth suicide. Finally, we need to honor and recognize those schools and communities who are taking positive steps towards preventing bullying and suicide, rather than just focusing on those where a tragedy has occurred.

In the end, suicide and bullying are both serious and pervasive issues for today's youth which we need to prevent. In order to do so, we need to understand, bullying alone does not cause suicide.

Stop Panicking About Bullies

Nick Gillespie

Nick Gillespie is the former editor-in-chief of Reason *magazine and the current editor of Reason.com and Reason.tv. He is the coauthor of* The Declaration of Independents: How Libertarian Politics Can Fix What's Wrong with America.

"When I was younger," a remarkably self-assured, soft-spoken 15-year-old kid named Aaron tells the camera, "I suffered from bullying because of my lips—as you can see, they're kind of unusually large. So I would kind of get [called] 'Fish Lips'—things like that a lot—and my glasses too, I got those at an early age. That contributed. And the fact that my last name is Cheese didn't really help with the matter either. I would get [called] 'Cheeseburger,' 'Cheese Guy'—things like that, that weren't really very flattering. Just kind of making fun of my name—I'm a pretty sensitive kid, so I would have to fight back the tears when I was being called names."

It's hard not to be impressed with—and not to like—young Aaron Cheese. He is one of the kids featured in the new Cartoon Network special "Stop Bullying: Speak Up," which premiered last week and is available online. I myself am a former geekish, bespectacled child whose lips were a bit too full, and my first name (as other kids quickly discovered) rhymes with two of the most-popular slang terms for male genitalia, so I also identified with Mr. Cheese. My younger years were filled with precisely the sort of schoolyard taunts that he recounts; they led ultimately to at least one fistfight and a lot of sour moods on my part.

As the parent now of two school-age boys, I also worry that my own kids will have to deal with such ugly and destructive behavior. And I welcome the common-sense antibul-lying strategies relayed in "Stop Bullying": Talk to your friends, your parents and your teachers. Recognize that you're not the problem. Don't be a silent witness to bullying.

What was once taken for granted—working the family farm, October tests with jack-o-lantern-themed ques-tions, hunting your own Easter eggs—is being threatened by paternalism run amok.

But is America really in the midst of a "bullying crisis," as so many now claim? I don't see it. I also suspect that our fears about the ubiquity of bullying are just the latest in a long line of well-intentioned yet hyperbolic alarms about how awful it is to be a kid today.

I have no interest in defending the bullies who dominate sandboxes, extort lunch money and use Twitter to taunt their classmates. But there is no growing crisis. Childhood and ado-lescence in America have never been less brutal. Even as the country's overprotective parents whip themselves up into a moral panic about kid-on-kid cruelty, the numbers don't point to any explosion of abuse. As for the rising wave of laws and regulations designed to combat meanness among students, they are likely to lump together minor slights with major of-fenses. The antibullying movement is already conflating seri-ous cases of gay-bashing and vicious harassment with things like . . . a kid named Cheese having a tough time in grade school.

How did we get here? We live in an age of helicopter par-ents so pushy and overbearing that Colorado Springs banned its annual Easter-egg hunt on account of adults jumping the starter's gun and scooping up treat-filled plastic eggs on behalf of their winsome kids. The Department of Education in New York City—once known as the town too tough for Al Ca-pone—is seeking to ban such words as "dinosaurs," "Halloween" and "dancing" from citywide tests on the grounds that they could "evoke unpleasant emotions in the students," it was reported this week. (Leave aside for the moment that perhaps the whole point of tests is to "evoke unpleasant emotions.")

And it's not only shrinking-violet city boys and girls who are being treated as delicate flowers. Early versions of new labor restrictions still being hashed out in Congress would have barred children under 16 from operating power-driven farm equipment and kept anyone under 18 from working at agricultural co-ops and stockyards (the latest version would let kids keep running machines on their parents' spreads). What was once taken for granted—working the family farm, October tests with jack-o-lantern-themed questions, hunting your own Easter eggs—is being threatened by paternalism run amok.

Now that schools are peanut-free, latex-free and soda-free, parents, administrators and teachers have got to worry about something. Since most kids now have access to cable TV, the Internet, unlimited talk and texting, college and a world of opportunities that was unimaginable even 20 years ago, it seems that adults have responded by becoming ever more overprotective and thin-skinned.

Kids might be fatter than they used to be, but by most standards they are safer and better-behaved than they were when I was growing up in the 1970s and '80s. Infant and adolescent mortality, accidents, sex and drug use—all are down from their levels of a few decades ago. Acceptance of homosexuality is up, especially among younger Americans. But given today's rhetoric about bullying, you could be forgiven for thinking that kids today are not simply reading and watching grim, postapocalyptic fantasies like "The Hunger Games" but actually inhabiting such terrifying terrain, a world where "Lord of the Flies" meets "Mad Max 2: The Road Warrior," presided over by Voldemort.

51

Even President Barack Obama has placed his stamp of approval on this view of modern childhood. Introducing the Cartoon Network documentary, he solemnly intones: "I care about this issue deeply, not just as the president, but as a dad. . . . We've all got more to do. Everyone has to take action against bullying."

One thing seems certain: The focus on bullying will lead to more lawsuits against schools and bullies, many of which will stretch the limits of empathy and patience.

The state of New Jersey was well ahead of the president. Last year, in response to the suicide of the 18-year-old gay Rutgers student Tyler Clementi, the state legislature passed "The Anti-Bullying Bill of Rights." The law is widely regarded as the nation's toughest on these matters. It has been called both a "resounding success" by Steve Goldstein, head of the gay-rights group Garden State Equality, and a "bureaucratic nightmare" by James O'Neill, the interim school superintendent of the township of Roxbury. In Congress, New Jersey Sen. Frank Lautenberg and Rep. Rush Holt have introduced the federal Tyler Clementi Higher Education Anti-Harassment Act.

The Foundation for Individual Rights in Education has called the Lautenberg-Holt proposal a threat to free speech because its "definition of harassment is vague, subjective and at odds with Supreme Court precedent." Should it become law, it might well empower colleges to stop some instances of bullying, but it would also cause many of them to be sued for repressing speech. In New Jersey, a school anti-bullying coordinator told the *Star-Ledger* that "The Anti-Bullying Bill of Rights" has "added a layer of paperwork that actually inhibits us" in dealing with problems. In surveying the effects of the law, the *Star-Ledger* reports that while it is "widely used and has helped some kids," it has imposed costs of up to $80,000 per school district for training alone and uses about 200 hours per month of staff time in each district, with some educators saying that the additional effort is taking staff "away from things such as substance-abuse prevention and college and career counseling."

One thing seems certain: The focus on bullying will lead to more lawsuits against schools and bullies, many of which will stretch the limits of empathy and patience. Consider, for instance, the current case of 19-year-old Eric Giray, who is suing New York's tony Calhoun School and a former classmate for $1.5 million over abuse that allegedly took place in 2004. Such cases can only become more common.

Which isn't to say that there aren't kids who face terrible cases of bullying. The immensely powerful and highly acclaimed documentary "Bully," whose makers hope to create a nationwide movement against the "bullying crisis," opens in selected theaters this weekend. The film follows the harrowing experiences of a handful of victims of harassment, including two who killed themselves in desperation. It is, above all, a damning indictment of ineffectual and indifferent school officials. No viewer can watch the abuse endured by kids such as Alex, a 13-year-old social misfit in Sioux City, Iowa, or Kelby, a 14-year-old lesbian in small-town Oklahoma, without feeling angry and motivated to change youth culture and the school officials who turn a blind eye.

It is stunning to learn that the most common locations for bullying are inside classrooms, in hallways and stairwells, and on playgrounds—areas ostensibly patrolled by teachers and administrators.

But is bullying—which the stopbullying.gov website of the Department of Health and Human Services defines as "teasing," "name-calling," "taunting," "leaving someone out on purpose," "telling other children not to be friends with someone," "spreading rumors about someone," "hitting/kicking/pinching," "spitting" and "making mean or rude hand gestures"—really a growing problem in America?

Despite the rare and tragic cases that rightly command our attention and outrage, the data show that things are, in fact, getting better for kids. When it comes to school violence, the numbers are particularly encouraging. According to the National Center for Education Statistics, between 1995 and 2009, the percentage of students who reported "being afraid of attack or harm at school" declined to 4% from 12%. Over the same period, the victimization rate per 1,000 students declined fivefold.

When it comes to bullying numbers, long-term trends are less clear. The makers of "Bully" say that "over 13 million American kids will be bullied this year," and estimates of the percentage of students who are bullied in a given year range from 20% to 70%. NCES changed the way it tabulated bullying incidents in 2005 and cautions against using earlier data. Its biennial reports find that 28% of students ages 12–18 reported being bullied in 2005; that percentage rose to 32% in 2007, before dropping back to 28% in 2009 (the most recent year for which data are available). Such numbers strongly suggest that there is no epidemic afoot (though one wonders if the new anti-bullying laws and media campaigns might lead to more reports going forward).

The most common bullying behaviors reported include being "made fun of, called names, or insulted" (reported by about 19% of victims in 2009) and being made the "subject of rumors" (16%). Nine percent of victims reported being "pushed, shoved, tripped, or spit on," and 6% reported being "threatened with harm." Though it may not be surprising that bullying mostly happens during the school day, it is stunning to learn that the most common locations for bullying are inside classrooms, in hallways and stairwells, and on playgrounds—areas ostensibly patrolled by teachers and administrators.

None of this is to be celebrated, of course, but it hardly paints a picture of contemporary American childhood as an unrestrained Hobbesian nightmare. Before more of our schools' money, time and personnel are diverted away from education in the name of this supposed crisis, we should make an effort to distinguish between the serious abuse suffered by the kids in "Bully" and the sort of lower-level harassment with which the Aaron Cheeses of the world have to deal.

In fact, Mr. Cheese, now a sophomore in high school with hopes of becoming a lawyer, provides a model in dealing with the sort of jerks who will always, unfortunately, be a presence in our schools. At the end of "Stop Bullying," he tells younger kids, "Just talk to somebody and I promise to you, it's going to get better." For Aaron, it plainly has: "It has been turned around actually. I am a generally liked guy. My last name has become something that's a little more liked. I have a friend named Mac and so together we are Mac and Cheese. That's cool."

Indeed, it is cool. And if we take a deep breath, we will realize that there are many more Aaron Cheeses walking the halls of today's schools than there are bullies. Our problem isn't a world where bullies are allowed to run rampant; it's a world where kids like Aaron are convinced that they are powerless victims.

CHAPTER 2

Is Cyberbullying
a Major Problem?

Chapter Preface

Cyberbullying, or online harassment, is dependent on technology. This means that the way the technology functions can have a major effect on whether, and to what extent, cyberbullying occurs. A software app like Secret for the iPhone, then, can potentially facilitate and encourage cyberbullying.

That at least has been the cause for some concern about Secret, according to Parker Marie Molloy who wrote about the app for *Bustle*. Molloy explains that the app allows users to post messages anonymously. Cofounder David Byttow compared the app to a "masquerade ball" where, he says, "You know who's on the guest list, but you don't know who is saying what."[1] Byttow says people will hear each other's "internal dialogues" and gain a sense of "belonging or validation."

Molloy, however, points out that in initial reviews of the app, users do not say they are validated. Instead they report that the app has been used for bullying and harassment. This is consistent with earlier apps that promised anonymity, such as PostSecret, a 2012 app that was discontinued after its developer realized it was being used for cyberbullying.

Cecilia Kang at *The Washington Post*, however, suggests that apps allowing anonymity have proliferated because there is a desire for them among teen users. Teens want to interact on social media, but they know that anything they say on Facebook or Twitter or other social media sites is permanently available. As Kang states, "They know that future employers and college recruiters are likely to sift carefully through their

---

1. Quoted in Parker Marie Molloy, "Secret, the Popular Message-Sharing App, Comes Under Fire Over Cyberbullying," *Bustle*, August 4, 2014. www.bustle.com/articles /34362-secret-the-popular-message-sharing-app-comes-under-fire-over-cyberbullying.

Twitter and Facebook accounts."[2] Anonymous apps allow teens to share information without having to worry about leaving a permanent record of everything they say or do.

Still, concerns about cyberbullying persist. Nick Bilton at *The New York Times* reports that many adults in Silicon Valley, where the Secret app debuted, have deleted it because it encourages abuse and cyberbullying—and, again, this is in a community of adults. Yik Yak, an app similar to Secret, decided to ban middle and high school students and to disable the app around schools after reports that it had been used for bullying and even for bomb threats. Secret, for its part, says it is going to add features to allow users to ban those who post abusive messages. Whether such fixes will be enough to prevent cyberbullying on the app is unclear.

The rest of this chapter discusses other issues of cyberbullying, such as whether cyberbullying is different than regular bullying and whether it is increasing or decreasing.

2. Cecilia Kang, "Seeking Privacy, Teens Turn to Anonymous-Messaging Apps," *Washington Post*, February 16, 2014. www.washingtonpost.com/business/technology/seeking
-privacy-teens-turn-to-anonymous-messaging-apps/2014/02/16/1ffa583a-9362-11e3
-b46a-5a3d0d2130da_story.html.

Cyberbullying Is Dangerous

Suzanne Phillips

Suzanne Phillips is adjunct professor of clinical psychology in the doctoral program of Long Island University and on the faculty of the postdoctoral programs of the Derner Institute of Adelphi University. She is the coauthor of Healing Together: A Couple's Guide to Coping with Trauma and Post-Traumatic Stress.

Once again cyberbullying has resulted in the suicide of a child.

This time the victim was Rebecca Sedwick, a 12-year-old girl who was at times "terrorized" by as many as 15 girls who ganged up on her and picked on her for months through on-line message boards and texts.

Despite the fact that Rebecca's parents changed her school, she, like other victims of cyberbullying, found that there was nowhere to hide. Cyberspace had become a dangerous place and cyberbullying had become lethal.

What Is Cyberbullying?

Cyberbullying is the use of internet or other digital devices such as E-mail, instant messaging, text messages, social networking sites, web pages, blogs, chat rooms or interactive game sites to send negative and harmful messages and images. While the term "Cyberbullying" is technically used when the victim or bully is a minor, it is also applied to the cyber harassment of college students.

According to Nancy Willard of the Center for Safe and Responsible Use of the Internet, cyberbullying can take the form of:

Flaming or online fighting with vulgar language

Harassment or repeated sending of mean and insulting messages

Denigration or demeaning gossip

Impersonation or pretending to be someone else and posting damaging messages

Outing or sharing someone's personal information or embarrassing secrets

Trickery or covertly drawing out and then exposing personal information

Exclusion or intentionally excluding someone from an inner on-line group or site

Cyber stalking or repeated frightening threats

The more that young people share their identities and thoughts on social networking sites, the more likely they are to be targets than those who do not use the sites.

Cyberbullying like any form of bullying is relational aggression. It is intended to make the victim feel frightened, humiliated, helpless and too often—hopeless. What makes cyber bullying particularly harmful and in the case of too many young people who have committed suicide, so deadly, is the nature and virulent reach of electronic medium.

- Cyberbullying is anonymous. Perpetrators can torture and harass without detection.

- Cyberbullying is relentless. It can be conducted 24/7 appearing constantly on the phone and computer that a young person uses on a daily basis for school and social connections.

- Cyberbullying assaults privacy boundaries in a way that magnifies the horror as it makes damaging material public to an infinite audience that can instantly download, save or forward to others.

Reported in *Cyber Bully: Bullying in a Digital Age*, David Knight, a high school student who found that a web page of negative, sexual accusations and negative descriptions about him had reached as far as Thailand, painfully describes, "Anyone with a computer can see it. . . . It doesn't go away when you come home from school. It makes me feel even more trapped."

Statistics reveal an increasing problem. Four in ten teens have experienced online bullying; girls are twice as likely to be victims *and* perpetrators, usually engaging in social sabotage of others; boys are more likely to target girls and less aggressive males; sexual and homophobic harassment is emerging as a prevalent aspect of cyberbullying; cyberbullying is most prevalent among 15 and 16 year olds; and the more that young people share their identities and thoughts on social networking sites, the more likely they are to be targets than those who do not use the sites.

In all types of bullying the role of the bystander is crucial—perhaps even more so in cyberbullying.

Why Teens Don't Tell

Electronic harassment is as real as and often more frightening than face-to-face bullying. Much like stalking or other types of assault the victim can often feel helpless, frozen, isolated, ashamed and not likely to reveal what is going on to parents or sometimes even to friends.

According to surveys, only 35% of cyberbullied teens and 51% of preteens told parents. The reasons given by teens in focus groups were fear of restriction from electronic use, fear of being blamed or expectation of parents' overreactions.

The answer for parents is not to ban a child or teen from their technological connections or to read every E-mail. Cyberspace is as much a viable social world as the playground, candy store or mall was to earlier generations.

- For parents, talking with children and teens about the forms of cyberbullying and strategies for dealing with it can be a valuable trusted collaboration. Supervision is different from invasion of privacy.

- For pre-teens and teens living at home or college students living with friends the answer in the face of harassing material or cyber terror is not to isolate and hide.

- You have done nothing wrong. You are entitled to the support of those around you.

- Work together and draw upon the guidelines listed below to respond to cyberbullying.

Guidelines for Responding to Cyberbullying

- Stop—Don't respond to the bully—even to the first offense—it only escalates the problem.

- Save the evidence—print copies and save the messages. Young children can be instructed to shut off the monitor if something upsetting appears (not the computer) and/or CALL YOU.

- Block the sender or point out how you can click the warning button on an instant message (IM) screen or chat screen that alerts the Internet Service Provider of objectionable material.

- As a parent if you and your child find that the perpetrator is another student, share evidence with the guidance counselor—even though 70% of the cyberbullying happens when a youngster is home, it often involves other students in the school.

- If the cyberbullying continues—contact the parents of the perpetrator. If you are comfortable with that, it can be very effective in helping everyone. Given that you have saved evidence, you can invite the need for steps to correct a dangerous situation for all.

- If needed contact an attorney to help you deal with the parents of the perpetrator.

- If the cyberbullying contains threats, intimidation, obscene material or sexual exploitation report it to the police or cyber crime unit in your area.

- Seek support and professional help for yourself and or your child if there is emotional stress reflected in depression, desperation, anxiety or thoughts of self-harm.

The Bystanders

As reflected in the title of Barbara Coloroso's book [*The Bully, the Bullied, and the Bystander*] on bullying, the cycle of this type of violence includes the bully, the bullied and the bystanders.

In all types of bullying the role of the bystander is crucial—perhaps even more so in cyberbullying.

If we overlook the ease with which our own children can unwittingly add to the horror of damaging someone's life by passing on the secrets, privacy or exposure of another with a simple click, we make cyberspace a dangerous place.

If as parents, we take stock of the amount of time and tenor of our children's face-to-face and on-line relationships—both friendly and unfriendly—we may be able to step in to help or get help for our own child who is acting like a bully or is frightened by a bully.

If we talk about and participate in steps with other parents, kids, school personnel and community members to underscore the power of the bystander to stop, delete, tell, block and report cyber assault, we change from bystanders to protectors. We re-establish safety. We never leave anyone in danger in cyberspace.

Female Cyberbullying Is a Serious Problem

Lori O. Favela

Lori O. Favela graduated from Liberty University in Lynchburg, Virginia, in 2014, with a concentration in teaching and learning.

In recent months, the epidemic of bullying in the United States has received widespread attention in the news media. Though bullying can be defined in many ways, researchers lean toward a definition that includes "aggression, intention, repetition and an imbalance of power between the aggressor and the victim" and also point out that bullying may be "direct, verbal, and indirect or relational," with well-known long-term effects on those involved. Although some claim that female aggression is on the decline and that the attention given recently to female cyberbullying is a "hoax" that is causing "panic," the truth is that female violence is a real and tangible concern that must be addressed. Girls, traditionally, have not been thought of as bullies in the definitional sense, although society is now becoming aware of the serious role of girls in bullying, their special characteristics, and unique methods of bullying, including the recent addition of cyberbullying to the already dangerous methods of relational bullying among females. A recent study by [S.] Hinduja and [J.W.] Patchin found that 25.8% of girls report having been cyberbullied, compared to only 16.8% of boys. An alarming 21.1% of girls report cyberbullying others, while only 18.3% of boys report the same. [N.E.] Werner, [M.F.] Bumpus, and [D.] Rock report that girls who are involved in relational bullying offline are more likely to participate in online bullying or to be victims of cyberbullying themselves. Girls are clearly at the forefront of this technological disaster.

Bullying and Status

Anthropologists have determined that bullying among males is a means of establishing a hierarchy and that bullying provides a sort of rite of passage to the males in the society. Goddard also notes that girls, though, also participate in bullying, but to gain male attention. Think of the movie *Mean Girls*; those beautiful girls with the most social power are the ones most into bullying in the school society. According to Goddard, psychologist Anthony Pellegrini states, "Bullying is a form of aggression and one that is used to deliberately secure resources". Typically, these "resources" are social status and peer adoration, of both the same and the opposite gender. Add to the mix the actual necessity of being technologically literate in 2010, and the concoction becomes lethal for girls: girls bully in more relational and indirect ways, and electronic communication makes this stealthy bullying even easier.

> *It is not enough to know the definition of cyberbullying, nor is it enough to know who perpetrates cyberbullying and how the aggression is committed.*

The venues for female cyberbullying are numerous. MySpace, Facebook, texting, IMing, and email are all common and easily accessible methods for covert bullying for both genders. Girls seem to be more drawn to these methods of bullying for several reasons: girls are not as concerned with establishing their dominance physically, girls prefer to utilize relational aggression (rumors, ostracizing one member, exclusion, etc.) as it fits better with female societal expectations, and girls prefer language use over other types of aggression, which is conducive to electronic means that rely on language use as the primary vehicle for the behavior. "Mean Girls" is in fact a sub-grouping of cyberbullies identified by Chisholm as specifically a group of females "targeting a victim."

Cyberbullying Examples

Examples of cyberbullying are as numerous as they are astounding. Recent examples of cyberbullying included the case of Megan Meier, who hanged herself after being bullied repeatedly on MySpace. Cyberbullies created an inflammatory webpage to terrorize Jodi Plumb, 15. On the site, she was criticized and threatened until she reported the page and it was removed. Most recently, Phoebe Prince, also 15, hanged herself after being cyberbullied on an amazing array of cyber venues, including even Twitter, and Craigslist. The list of cyberbullied teens is long and agonizing and the cyberbullying, while often created by girls, isn't always directed only at females. Even males experience intense and debilitating cyberbullying.

The experience of cyberbullying is possibly intensified from the experience of the playground bully for several reasons: the target's experience appears to be intensified because the perpetrator can hide behind a screen name, and can act without fear of punishment. In addition, the audience is not merely the playground inhabitants, but is impossibly huge, spanning states, countries, cultures, and even time.

It is not enough to know the definition of cyberbullying, nor is it enough to know who perpetrates cyberbullying and how the aggression is committed. Prevention and protection of the innocent is the goal of this article.

Addressing Female Cyberbullying

So, what can schools do about cyberbullying, particularly among female students? The following outline suggests practical and usable ideas and strategies that address at least some of the cyberbullying attacks that seem to be most common.

1. An Acceptable Use Policy (AUP) for internet, blogs, podcasts and social networking sites should be crafted and signed by all stakeholders. Although most districts and schools already have such policies, care should be taken to ensure that there is also a provision that no student should post information about other students, especially malicious and false information. Finally, schools should ensure that there is also a provision against student posting of any information that allows others to identify a student or his/her location.

It still makes sense to instruct parents to keep an eye on their children's internet use patterns. Even a little precaution can go a long way.

---

2. Telling a trusted adult is a common idea for a solution, but, often, this track makes the situation worse. Several researchers have noted that cyberbullying causes distraction in all students, victims, perpetrators, and by-standers alike, as well as in teachers and administrators, taking minds from valuable class time. Involving even more people in the cyberbullying adds fuel to an already dangerous fire. Teaching students to respond to the bullying with humor, or by ignoring the attack, may be a better option, according to Mary Muscari of Binghamton University. Psychologist Izzy Kalman also endorses staying away from getting the bully in "trouble" with police or school administrators, which often makes the bullying worse. Kalman advises to follow the biblical principles of "turning the other cheek" or "treating others as you would like to be treated" . . . *especially* over the internet. Kalman says that "Being nice to others is the best guarantee that people will be nice to you." "Netiquette" should be taught, in specific terms, to all users of the internet.

3. If deemed appropriate and necessary, reporting of cyberviolence can be done in several ways:

- CyberTipline: Unsolicited, obscene materials and/or threats can be reported to http://www.missingkids.com/cybertip/ or by calling 1-800-843-5678.

- ISP: Report harassment to the bully's internet service provider [ISP] and request that the offender's account be suspended or blocked. Violations can also be reported to www.whois.com.

- Police: Contact and report cyberbullying to local police, especially if the bully threatens violence or abduction

- School: Report cyberbullying to school, especially when any school-related content is involved.

4. Although some researchers have found that parental control of students' internet use has little effect on cyberbullying, it still makes sense to instruct parents to keep an eye on their children's internet use patterns. Even a little precaution can go a long way. Instruct kids to keep personal information private, and to keep passwords private (except from parents). Teach children to refrain from sharing secrets, photos, or anything embarrassing. Inform students to avoid sending messages when they are angry to avoid regret, and teach kids to be good "cyberfriends" by refraining from sending emails or IMs written by a friend to anyone else without permission.

5. Finally, individual schools need to address more complex issues at their own institutions. Ronald Jacobson, a researcher at the University of Washington proposes that schools might be able to help the bully no longer want to bully. The idea is that the bully and the victim lack the social skills for peaceful coexistence.

Programs for individual schools that address these more global issues are available at several websites, and the program Teen Talking Circles has been chosen as an example program that is appropriate to address cyberbullying in that school's particular context. Creating avenues for girls to learn and practice appropriate communication can help.

- Teen Talking Circles have the objectives of "educating, inspiring, and empowering young women . . . fostering partnerships among genders, generations and cultures, and by providing support for youth in positive self-expression and social action for a just, compassionate and sustainable world." These objectives meet exactly the needs of the Academy in that the prevention of cyberbullying is best accomplished by meeting the specific needs of the institution.

- Other suggestions include teaching the adults to be aware of their own relational aggression (eye-rolling, facial expressions, etc. . . .); girls pick up on these cues quote readily. Other suggestions include providing and encouraging physical activity to support body image and self-esteem, and to provide many opportunities for all manners of healthy female relationships.

The Cyberbullying Problem Is Overhyped

Tim Cushing

Tim Cushing is a regular contributor to Techdirt.com.

Cyberbullying continues to be the topic du jour, especially for school administrators and legislators, both of which feel something needs to be done, even if they both have nothing in the form of hard data showing the threat matches the perception.

Exaggerated Problem

The result is bad policies and worse laws aimed at fighting an exaggerated problem. How exaggerated is it? Well, that depends on who you ask. As Larry Magid at HuffPo [*Huffington Post*] points out, the numbers tend to rise if there's a product or service in play.

> I got a call recently from a woman who works for a company that makes an app designed to "keep kids safe" by enabling parents to monitor their texts and social media activities. The pitch included some dire statistics such as "70 percent of kids are cyberbullied" and—like other companies that make parental-control software—I was also told that it helps protect kids from strangers who would do them harm.

> Actual studies point to much lower numbers, although there's no solid consensus.

> The National Center for Educational Statistics reports that 6 percent of students in grades 6–12 experienced cyberbullying. The Centers for Disease Control found in 2011 that

16.2 percent of students had been bullied via email, chat rooms, instant messaging, websites or texting—compared to 20.1 percent who had been bullied on school property (traditional bullying)—during the 12 months prior to the survey. The Cyberbullying Research Center reports that "on average, about 24 percent of the students who have been a part of our last six studies have said they have been the victim of cyberbullying at some point in their lifetime."

Dan Olweus, who the editor of the *European Journal of Development Psychology* referred to as the "father of bullying research," wrote a 2012 article for that journal where he said that "claims about cyberbullying made in the media and elsewhere are greatly exaggerated and have little empirical scientific support." Based on a three-year survey of more than 440,000 U.S. children (between 3rd and 12th grade), 4.5 percent of kids had been cyberbullied compared to 17.6 percent from that same sample who had experienced traditional bullying. An even more interesting statistic from that study is that only 2.8 percent of kids had bullied others.

Kids, due to their inherent lack of a developed world view, say "mean or hurtful" things all the time. Trying to portray this as "evidence" of widespread bullying is disingenuous.

Because cyberbullying isn't precisely defined, variations are to be expected. But even the most expansive definitions fail to return the scary numbers quoted by those pushing software, policies and legislation.

A Vested Interest

i-Safe, "the leader in Internet safety education," compiled these cyberbullying numbers back in 2004 (and hasn't updated them in nearly a decade).

42% of kids have been bullied while online. 1 in 4 have had it happen more than once.

35% of kids have been threatened online. Nearly 1 in 5 have had it happen more than once.

21% of kids have received mean or threatening e-mail or other messages.

58% of kids admit someone has said mean or hurtful things to them online. More than 4 out of 10 say it has happened more than once.

53% of kids admit having said something mean or hurtful to another person online. More than 1 in 3 have done it more than once.

58% have not told their parents or an adult about something mean or hurtful that happened to them online.

The most surprising thing about these numbers is that the "mean or hurtful" stat isn't closer to 100%. Kids, due to their inherent lack of a developed world view, say "mean or hurtful" things all the time. Trying to portray this as "evidence" of widespread bullying is disingenuous. i-Safe may be a nonprofit, but it still sells subscriptions to instructional software through its website. i-Safe has a vested interest in portraying bullying as worse than it actually is.

SafetyNETkids, which also sells videos and curriculum, has this stat (among others) on its website:

Around half of teens have been the victims of cyber bullying.

This startling "fact" is quoted all over the internet and is supposedly pulled from a *Hartford County Examiner* article. Unfortunately, that stat shows up nowhere in the referenced article and the study itself was performed not by the *Examiner*, but by the National Crime Prevention Council [NCPC], home of McGruff the Crime Dog. The actual "stat" quoted by the *Examiner* says simply, "over 40% of all teenagers with Internet access have reported being bullied online." At some point, someone decided "over 40%" meant "around half," which sounds much more epidemic.

Focusing on the technology—instead of the child's social emotional state—is likely to divert their attention from real issues.

The actual number contained in the NCPC's report is *43%*, closer to 40% than "almost half." How did this study manage to come up with a higher percentage than the others Magid quotes? By applying some very loose definitions, much like i-Safe above.

Most commonly, bullying is thought of as a pervasive, consistent activity, not a one-time event. Dan Olweus, "father of bullying research," defines bullying as "aggressive behavior that is intentional and that invoices an imbalance of power. Most often, it is repeated over time." Recent studies like those performed by the NCPC and deployed by i-Safe have upped the number of incidents by weakening the term. While someone *might* feel "bullied" by a one-off interaction, defining every singular experience as "bullying" dilutes the meaning, leading to the punishment of non-bullies and diverting resources from dealing with real problems.

There are a lot of reasons why exaggerating is bad. For one thing, it causes parents to worry unnecessarily. Of course parents are concerned about their kids use of online technology but focusing on the technology—instead of the child's social emotional state—is likely to divert their attention from real issues. And, as Olweus pointed out in this paper, "It may also create feelings of powerlessness and helplessness in the face of the presumably 'huge' and ubiquitous cyberbullying problem . . . [and] that fixating on cyberbullying could encourage an unfortunate shift in the focus of anti-bullying work if digital bullying is seen as the key bullying problem in the schools."

Anti-Bullying Policies Make Things Worse

Some research exists indicating that the expansion of anti-bullying policies is making things worse.

University of Texas at Arlington criminologist Seokjin Jeong analyzed data collected from 7,000 students from all 50 states.

He thought the results would be predictable and would show that anti-bullying programs curb bullying. Instead—he found the opposite.

Jeong said it was, "A very disappointing and a very surprising thing. Our anti-bullying programs, either intervention or prevention does not work."

The study concluded that students at schools with anti-bullying programs might actually be more likely to become a victim of bullying. It also found that students at schools with no bullying programs were less likely to become victims.

The results were stunning for Jeong. "Usually people expect an anti-bullying program to have some impact—some positive impact."

The downside . . . is that real problems are being ignored while legislators and school administrators chase down incidents common to any group of people interacting with each other, especially children and teens.

---

i-Safe says 42% have been bullied online, but only 25% have had it happen "more than once." 58% have had something "mean or hurtful" said to them, but only 40% have seen repeat occurrences. There's a huge gap between these single events and pervasive behavior and that gap is being exploited.

The detailed methodology from the Harris Poll powering the NCPC's bullying numbers is no longer posted at its site, but the four-page summary uses the following to define "bullying."

- Someone pretending to be someone else in order to trick them online, getting them to reveal personal information.

- Someone lying about someone online.

- Pretending to be them while communicating with someone else.

- Posting unflattering pictures of them online, without permission.

Between the weak definitions and the inclusion of one-time events, NCPC has watered down "bullying" to define actions that, while temporarily unpleasant and/or embarrassing, are hardly evidence of "aggressive behavior repeated over time."

This isn't to say that cyberbullying doesn't exist and isn't a problem. This is simply to point out that the more worrisome the numbers presented, the more likely there's a narrative or product being pushed that benefits those doing the pushing. The downside, as noted by Olweus above, is that real problems are being ignored while legislators and school administrators chase down incidents common to any group of people interacting with each other, *especially* children and teens.

Cyberbullying Is Less Common than Traditional Bullying

American Psychological Association

The American Psychological Association is a scientific professional organization of psychologists in the United States and Canada.

Traditional in-person bullying is far more common than cyberbullying among today's youth and should be the primary focus of prevention programs, according to research findings presented at the American Psychological Association's [APA] 120th Annual Convention.

Focus on Traditional Bullying

"Claims by the media and researchers that cyberbullying has increased dramatically and is now the big school bullying problem are largely exaggerated," said psychologist Dan Olweus, PhD, of the University of Bergen, Norway. "There is very little scientific support to show that cyberbullying has increased over the past five to six years, and this form of bullying is actually a less frequent phenomenon."

APA presented Olweus at the convention with its 2012 Award for Distinguished Contributions to Research in Public Policy for his 40 years of research and intervention in the area of bullying among youth.

To demonstrate that cyberbullying is less frequent than "traditional" bullying, Olweus cited several large-scale studies he conducted, including one involving approximately 450,000 U.S. students in grades three to 12. In the latter, regular surveys were conducted in connection with the introduction of Olweus's bullying prevention program in 1,349 schools from 2007 to 2010. Another study followed 9,000 students in grades four through 10 in 41 schools in Oslo, Norway, from 2006 to 2010.

In the U.S. sample, an average of 18 percent of students said they had been verbally bullied, while about 5 percent said they had been cyberbullied. About 10 percent said they had bullied others verbally and 3 percent said they had cyberbullied others. Similarly, in the Norwegian sample, 11 percent said they had been verbally bullied, 4 percent reported being the victim of cyberbullying, 4 percent said they had verbally bullied others and 1 percent said they had cyberbullied others.

To be cyberbullied or to cyberbully other students seems to a large extent to be part of a general pattern of bullying where use of electronic media is only one possible form, and, in addition, a form with low prevalence.

Other analyses showed that 80 percent to 90 percent of cyberbullied students were also exposed to traditional forms of bullying—that is, they were bullied verbally, physically or in more indirect, relational ways, such as being the subject of false, mean rumors. Similarly, most cyberbullies also bullied in more traditional ways.

All students filled out the Olweus Bullying Questionnaire, which asks extensive questions about an individual's experience with bullying, both as a victim and a perpetrator. The survey includes questions about the students' experience with cyberbullying, which is defined as taking place via a mobile phone or the Internet.

Few New Victims

"These results suggest that the new electronic media have actually created few 'new' victims and bullies," Olweus said. "To be cyberbullied or to cyberbully other students seems to a large extent to be part of a general pattern of bullying where use of electronic media is only one possible form, and, in addition, a form with low prevalence."

This is not to say that cyberbullying cannot be a problem in schools and outside of school, Olweus noted. Cyberbullied children, like targets of more traditional bullying, often suffer from depression, poor self-esteem, anxiety and even suicidal thoughts, he said.

"However, it is difficult to know to what extent these problems actually are a consequence of cyberbullying itself. As we've found, this is because the great majority of cyberbullied children and youth are also bullied in traditional ways, and it is well documented that victims of traditional bullying suffer from the bad treatment they receive," he said. "Nonetheless, there are some forms of cyberbullying—such as having painful or embarrassing pictures or videos posted—which almost certainly have negative effects. It is therefore important also to take cyberbullying seriously both in research and prevention."

Olweus recommends that schools and communities invest time and technical efforts in anonymously disclosing identified cases of cyberbullying—and then communicating clearly and openly the results to the students. This strategy can substantially increase the perceived risk of disclosure and is likely to reduce further the already low prevalence of cyberbullying, he said.

"Given that traditional bullying is much more prevalent than cyberbullying, it is natural to recommend schools to direct most of their efforts to counteracting traditional bullying. I don't want to trivialize or downplay cyberbullying but I definitely think it is necessary and beneficial to place cyberbullying in proper context and to have a more realistic picture of its prevalence and nature," he said.

The Links Between Cyberbullying and Suicide Are Oversimplified

Alison Auld

Alison Auld is a journalist with the Canadian Press.

The stories pop up on Carol Todd's computer with distressing regularity.

They are tales with an eerily similar template that chronicle the suicides of young people who often had endured the torment of prolonged and relentless online bullying.

In ways, they are much like the story of her own daughter Amanda, a 15-year-old Grade 10 student who took her life a year ago [2012] following months of harassment at school and online over images posted on the Internet of her body.

"Bullycide": An Oversimplication

One of the threads tying their deaths together is a cause-and-effect link made by the media, politicians and parents between persistent bullying and the victim's decision to end their life—a phenomenon that generated its own buzzword—"bullycide."

It is something Todd and health experts say oversimplifies teen suicide and cyberbullying at the expense of recognizing the complex set of mental health issues that are usually at play in many cases.

"Amanda's story, when you look at all the different pieces, it's very complicated," Todd said from her home in Port Coquitlam, B.C., adding that her daughter had a learning disability that affected her coping skills.

"I don't really like it when they say Amanda was cyberbullied to death. That wasn't the case and I don't think there's enough supports for kids for mental health issues, which is ultimately why they take their own lives."

Todd's death was one of several that spurred governments across the country to sit up and respond to what was being portrayed as a worsening problem for young people who couldn't easily escape the potential anguish of the online world.

In Nova Scotia, 17-year-old Rehtaeh Parsons was taken off life-support after a suicide attempt last April [2013] that her family said was brought on by months of bullying. The family said she was harassed after a digital photograph of her allegedly being sexually assaulted was circulated.

Being cyberbullied can be the straw that broke the camel's back, but the media and politicians at times simplify the issue to bullying equals suicide.

Jamie Hubley, an openly gay Ontario teenager, wrote in a suicide note of the pain of bullying and depression before taking his life in 2011.

The cases, among others in the U.S., shone an intense light on cyberbullying and its effects on young people, receiving widespread media coverage and prompting calls for government action.

Mental Health Overlooked

Dr. Jitender Sareen, a psychiatrist and professor at the University of Manitoba, says much of the coverage gave the facile notion that cyberbullying causes suicide, overlooking possible mental-health issues.

"Being cyberbullied can be the straw that broke the camel's back, but the media and politicians at times simplify the issue to bullying equals suicide," he said in Winnipeg.

"The vast majority of people who get bullied don't die by suicide, just like in hockey the number of people who get concussed don't die by suicide."

Sareen uses the example of someone with a lung disorder who then dies from a common cold to explain that many young people who take their own lives after being bullied had mental-health issues that affected their coping skills.

A 2012 study of 41 cases of teen suicides found that 32 per cent of the teens had a mood disorder, while another 15 per cent had depression symptoms.

Kelly McBride, a media ethicist at the Florida-based Poynter Institute, wrote in a blunt October [2013] post that by simplifying the issues, journalists perpetuated inaccurate information about suicides and bullying.

"When journalists . . . imply that teenage suicides are directly caused by bullying, we reinforce a false narrative that has no scientific support," she wrote. "In doing so, we miss opportunities to educate the public about the things we could be doing to reduce both bullying and suicide."

Tim Wall, executive director of the Canadian Association for Suicide Prevention, says that focusing on cyberbullying prevents discussion of other broader issues related to mental health. The barrage of coverage of teen suicides also takes away attention from other groups and their mental health challenges, he says.

"We have a population that is aging rapidly, so that suicide rate is just going to go up and up and we are not talking about that because so much of the attention is being focused just in this one area," he said.

"If we put all of our attention on this one issue of bullying then we're going to miss all the other things that are also contributing to it, so it requires a multi-pronged approach."

Education Before Legislation

In the wake of Parsons' death, the Nova Scotia government introduced the Cyber-Safety Act, which allows people to try to restrict the cyberbully and sue if they or their children are cyberbullied.

Cyberbullying expert and Dalhousie University law professor Wayne MacKay says the issue stretches beyond government and law enforcement. MacKay served as chairman of a task force that submitted a report in February 2012 to the Nova Scotia government on bullying.

Experts and parents say the response needs to reach beyond punitive, legislative change and work on improving kids' mental health and their coping skills.

The report dismissed the suggestion that there is a rise in teen suicides and strongly cautioned against making the link between cyberbullying and suicide.

"It's really important to not in any way popularize or glamorize (suicide), which then can lead to a kind of bizarre copycat effect," he said in an interview.

The report included seven recommendations on mental health interventions, including having schools linked with psychiatrists and training youth workers on identifying suicide risks. Many of those have been acted on.

Experts and parents say the response needs to reach beyond punitive, legislative change and work on improving kids' mental health and their coping skills, while boosting mental health resources for youth.

"It's not just about legislation," said Todd, adding that her daughter died on World Mental Health Day. "Legislation is the end piece—there's all the education and prevention before that."

Wall agrees, saying governments haven't found their footing completely when it comes to addressing the problem.

"We haven't yet caught up to this issue of cyberbullying in terms of developing a comprehensive response to it," he said. "My hope is that we'll be involved in a national forum to look specifically at the issue and how we can address it."

Cyberbullying Is Serious but Not an Epidemic

Larry Magid

Larry Magid is a journalist and technology columnist and the author of Child Safety on the Information Highway.

I'm glad that media outlets and public officials are shining a light on cyberbullying and bullying in general. It's important to pay attention to this serious problem, but we need to keep it in perspective. As bad as it is, cyberbullying is not an epidemic and it's not killing our children.

Rates Not Rising

Yes, it's probably one of the more widespread youth risks on the Internet and yes there are some well publicized horrific cases of cyberbullying victims who have committed suicide, but let's look at this in context.

Bullying has always been a problem among adolescents and, sadly, so has suicide. In the few known cases of suicide after cyberbullying, there are likely other contributing factors. That's not to diminish the tragedy or suggest that the cyberbullying didn't play a role but—as with all online youth risk, we need to look at what else was going on in the child's life. Even when a suicide or other tragic event does occur, cyberbullying is often accompanied by a pattern of offline bullying and sometimes there are other issues including depression, problems at home, and self-esteem issues.

"Suicide," said psychologist Dr. Patti Agatston, "is a complex and multifaceted act that is the result of a combination of factors in any individual. What we need to learn more about is what are the protective factors, since many youth are bullied and do not engage in suicidal behaviors." Agatston is a board member of the International Bullying Prevention Association (IBPA) that's planning an upcoming conference themed "Bullying and Intolerance: From Risk to Resiliency?"

One thing we know about cyberbullying is that it's often associated with real-world bullying.

While there is increased awareness of the dangers of bullying and rightful concern over suicide, the percentage of youth who report being physically bullied actually decreased between 2003 and 2008 from 22% to 15%, according to a peer reviewed study published in the *Archives of Pediatric and Adolescent Medicine*. And before making any assumptions about technology contributing to teen suicide, take a look at government data that shows (with the exception of 2004) a slight gradual decline in teen suicide rates from the 1990s to 2008.

Certain populations—especially gay, lesbian and transgender (LGBT) youth—experience a significantly higher rate of bullying. An Iowa State University study found that 54% of LGBT youth had been victims of cyberbullying within the past 30 days. 45% of the respondents "reported feeling depressed as a result of being cyberbullied," according to the study's authors. 38% felt embarrassed, and 28% felt anxious about attending school. The authors reported that "more than a quarter (26%) had suicidal thoughts."

Numbers Don't Show a Cyberbullying Epidemic

Research from the Cyberbullying Research Center indicates that about one in five teens have been cyberbullied at least once in their lifetimes and 10% in the past 30 days. That's bad, but not an epidemic. A 2010 study by Cox Communications came up with numbers similar to those from the Cyberbullying Research Center, finding that approximately 19 percent of teens say they've been cyberbullied online or via text message and 10 percent say they've cyberbullied someone else. Partly because there is no single accepted definition of cyberbullying, you will find other numbers that are much higher and much lower.

One thing we know about cyberbullying is that it's often associated with real-world bullying. A UCLA [University of California Los Angeles] study found that 85 percent of those bullied online were also bullied at school.

It may seem counterintuitive but research has shown that exaggeration and scare tactics can actually increase risk. Exaggerating bullying makes it like it's normal: "Everyone does it so it must be OK." Norms research from Professors H. Wesley Perkins and David Craig has shown that emphasizing that most kids don't bully actually decreases bullying. As Cyberbullying Research Center co-director Justin Patchin said in my CBS News/CNET podcast, kids have a tendency to way overestimate the percentage of kids who bully. . . . When reporting on suicide risk, it's important for media to study guidelines and be senstive to risk of copycat suicides.

The most commonly recognized definition of bullying includes repeated, unwanted aggressive behavior over a period of time with an imbalance of power between the bully and the victim. In theory, that also covers cyberbullying, but some have taken a broader approach to cyberbullying to also include single or occasional episodes of a person insulting another person online. Indeed, because of the possibility of it being forwarded, a single episode of online harassment can have long-term consequences. "'Power' and 'repetition' may be manifested a bit differently online than in traditional bullying," Susan Limber, professor of psychology at Clemson University, said in an interview that appeared in a publication of the U.S. Department of Education's Office of Safe and Drug-Free Schools. She added, "a student willing to abuse technology can easily wield great power over his or her target just by having the ability to reach a large audience, and often by hiding his or her identity."

Parents and authorities need to avoid jumping to immediate conclusions until they understand the severity of an incident.

Manifestations of cyberbullying include name calling, sending embarrassing pictures, sharing personal information or secrets without permission, and spreading rumors. It can also include trickery, exclusion, and impersonation.

Not All Bullying Is Equally Harmful

Some have a much broader definition of cyberbullying that can include any type of mean or rude comment, even if it's not particularly hurtful or traumatic.

When talking about bullying and cyberbullying, it's important to remember that not every incident is equally harmful. There are horrendous cases where children are terribly hurt but there are many cases where kids are able to handle it themselves. That's not to say it's ever right—there is never an excuse for being mean—but parents and authorities need to avoid jumping to immediate conclusions until they understand the severity of an incident. And, of course, different children will react differently to incidents depending on a number of factors including their own physiological makeup, vulnerability and resiliency.

It's not always obvious if a child is a victim of cyberbullying, but some possible signs include: suddenly being reluctant to go online or use a cell phone; avoiding a discussion about what they're doing online; depression, mood swings, change in eating habits; and aloofness or a general disinterest in school and activities. A child closing the browser or turning off the cell phone when a parent walks in the room can be a sign of cyberbullying, though it can also be a sign of other issues including an inappropriate relationship or just insistence on privacy.

There are no silver bullets but at ConnectSafely.org (a site I help operate) we came up with a number of tips including: don't respond, don't retaliate; talk to a trusted peer or adult; and save the evidence. We also advise young people to be civil toward others and not to be bullies themselves. Finally, "be a friend, not a bystander." Don't forward mean messages and let bullies know that their actions are not cool.

Act but Don't Overreact

If your child is cyberbullied, don't start by taking away his or her Internet privileges. That's one reason kids often don't talk about Net-related problems with parents. Instead, try to get your child to calmly explain what has happened. If possible, talk with the parents of the other kids involved and, if necessary, involve school authorities. If the impact of the bullying spills over to school (as it usually does), the school has a right to intervene.

CHAPTER 3

Current
CONTROVERSIES

What Types of People Are Targeted for Bullying?

Chapter Preface

Students with disabilities can face particularly fierce bullying in school, according to the National Bullying Prevention Center. Though research on this topic has been limited, the ten studies that have been done in the United States suggest that children with disabilities are bullied twice or three times as much as other students. One study showed that 60 percent of children with disabilities were bullied, as opposed to 25 percent of children without disabilities. A briefing paper written by Jonathan Young, Ari Ne'eman, and Sara Gelser for the National Council on Disability notes that children with disabilities are often targeted directly because of their disability. The authors claimed, "Evidence suggests that the response of policymakers, educators and researchers to the bullying of students with disabilities has not been nearly sufficient to address the breadth or gravity of the problem."[1]

One student who faced intense bullying at school because of a disability was Molly Burke. Burke had problems with her vision from birth, but she lost her sight completely at the age of thirteen. Rather than supporting her, the school and her friends began to target and stigmatize her. Burke was unusually able to get around for a blind person—she has a rare, limited ability to "hear" objects, which functions somewhat like sonar or echolocation in bats. As a result, her schoolmates decided she was faking blindness. As Sydney Loney explained in an article in *Chatelaine*:

> On Molly's grade 8 school trip to Ottawa, the friends she'd planned to share a room with no longer wanted her in it. When her teachers assigned her to the room anyway, the

---

1. Jonathan Young, Ari Ne'eman, and Sara Gelser, "Bullying and Students with Disabilities," National Council on Disability, March 9, 2011. www.ncd.gov/publications/2011/March92011.

girls made her sleep under a desk. Molly turned 14 on the trip, and her roommates promised to make her look pretty. She couldn't see that instead of applying makeup, they wrote on her face, and the "product" they put in her hair was whipped cream. "At that point, I felt so low that I didn't have the confidence to stand up for myself. I wasn't good at confrontation, and I felt cornered." Molly went to her guidance counsellor for help, only to be told she had brought the bullying on herself. "That's when I really realized I was in a bad situation: Not only was I being bullied, but nobody believed me."[2]

The bullying got worse, and Burke contemplated suicide and had to change schools. Eventually she found a school where she was supported. After graduation, she worked with the organization Me to We and began speaking about bullying at schools. Her goal is to help prevent the kind of harassment to which she was subjected because of her disability.

The rest of this chapter examines other groups that are singled out for bullying, including immigrants, exceptionally bright kids, LGBT (lesbian, gay, bisexual, and transgender) children, and those with autism, among others. The viewpoints presented demonstrate that there are many aspects of the bullying phenomenon.

2. Sydney Loney, "Blind and Bullied: She Lost Her Sight and Then Things Got Worse," *Chatelaine*, March 22, 2013. www.chatelaine.com/living/real-life-stories/blind-and-bullied-teenage-activist-molly-burke-shares-her-inspirational-story.

Bullied Boys: Why Bright Lads Are Being Picked On

The Independent

The Independent *is a daily British newspaper.*

Tommy Stenton was a bright boy who lived through hell in his last year of primary school and his first year at secondary school. The reason was that he was quiet and studious, so the other children picked on him for showing them up.

"What happened was that we moved and I had to change schools and I had no friends, so I was just keeping my head down and getting on with my books when it started. It was name-calling and people pushing and shoving me around. Also, the teacher didn't help. She used to say to the other kids that they weren't doing as much work as me and they'd have to stay in at break, and they didn't like that so they used to call me all sorts of things, like boffin and geek."

Tommy quickly started to hide his interest in his schoolwork. "I decided if I didn't do as well they wouldn't pick on me as much, so I used to try harder to get stuff wrong and act more stupid. I wasn't at the top of the class, and I wasn't at the bottom. Then, when I went up to secondary school, no one noticed because by then it was who I was."

It was Tommy's elder sister who found out how badly he was doing, recognised that it was out of character and told his teachers. "And after that it just got sorted." His teachers encouraged him, he grew in confidence and found friends of an equal intelligence. Now, at 15, he is happy at Danum School Technology College, an 11–18 comprehensive near Doncaster. He is predicted to get 11 GCSEs [an academic qualification in

Britain based on testing] and hopes to do physics, chemistry and maths at A-level and become a teacher.

Natalie, 16, who lives in the South-east (and doesn't want to give her surname), is hoping that things will turn out as well for her younger brother Will, 11, who, like her, has been bullied for being clever. "He'd come home from primary school and run straight up to his room because he didn't want us to see he was upset. And it's a lot worse for guys, they often don't have the same social skills as girls."

A recent study of gifted children in nine state secondary schools . . . has confirmed that clever pupils, especially boys, can be bullied and will "dumb down" to fit in.

Will is now in secondary school and has his girl twin and two older sisters looking out for him. "If we see anything happening, we go over and say 'You alright, Will?' and that usually sorts it."

But Natalie knows how important it is to get things sorted. From about nine she was bullied for being smart and speaking up in class. She was called names and had "lesbian" pictures planted in her bag. "So you start not answering questions, not writing things down, and not doing as well as you should do. There's always pressure not to perform well, and everyone wants to be popular and go along with the majority."

Despite this she managed to do well in her GCSEs, and is aiming for a career in psychology or criminology. "You come to realise that the bullies are going to be the ones that fail. My dad knows this. He was the only person in his road to go to grammar school and he got rinsed for it, but he saw that everyone else was still going to be there in 30 years' time, and they are. He's the only one who got out."

A recent study of gifted children in nine state secondary schools, by researchers at Roehampton University, has confirmed that clever pupils, especially boys, can be bullied and will "dumb down" to fit in. Being funny, good at sports and having a more disruptive pupil as a friend also helps. "Some pupils are able to maintain popularity with peers in spite of their high academic achievement," says Becky Francis, professor of education. "What appears to be a fundamental facilitator of this is their physical appearance, and for boys, their physical ability at sport."

Bullying the class "swot" has always been popular, but today's pupils say that the popularity of American high-school films, which often feature stereotypical boy geeks, has made it worse. They say that in "ordinary" state schools it often feels as if there aren't other intelligent pupils around, and they believe that teachers make it worse by not realising that bullying is going on.

"We discovered that the main thing that made our pupils uncomfortable was to be seen winning things," says Fran Baker, assistant head at Edenham High School, an 11–16 comprehensive in Croydon that is successfully tackling bullying. "Often the teasing and bullying comes from children who know they aren't going to be the ones winning things. Disaffected pupils have low self-esteem and try to bring down the other children to their level."

As a result of talking to students, the school now has an honours system that rewards pupils for things besides academic achievement and has used a programme run by the charity Beatbullying to help change the culture, "which has been amazing. Obviously, we've known for quite some time that children get bullied for being geeky and nerdy," says Sarah Dyer, new media director and spokesperson for Beatbullying, "but all the research shows that over 50 per cent of young people in the UK are affected by bullying which means an absolutely huge impact of achievement if millions of children are dumbing down and not meeting their target attainments."

Beatbullying believes effective bullying prevention programmes can be set up in schools for £4 for each pupil. "Plenty of schools have poor programmes, but a good one is properly embedded and sustained. Once we implement a programme we return to it every three to six months and we are always looking ahead to things like training the next generation of peer mentors. This money is a drop in the ocean, but the Government still doesn't get it, even though it's prepared to spend £23m to combat knife and gun crime."

One key to change would be "for teachers to pick up on bullying more."

Beatbullying has just launched a national "cyber mentor" scheme, which allows pupils to access help online. The scheme has 850 mentors aged 11 to 25 and 25,000 pupils accessed it in its first month of operation. "We have absolutely smashed our targets already," says Sarah Dyer. "Young people love that they don't have to see anyone face-to-face. And boys especially have said that it wouldn't make any difference to them if their cyber mentor was a girl because there's no physical meeting."

For Natalie, who is a young cyber mentor, one key to change would be "for teachers to pick up on bullying more, but often they just want to get the lesson done and don't want to be bothered that only one person's answering all the questions. And maybe teachers could be more strict, or could stream children from a younger age."

Tommy Stenton thinks parents also need to change. "You need to know how your child is, and if you see a change then ask about it."

The bullying of "geeks", he says, goes on everywhere. "It's exactly the same in every school. It's so stupid. It gets people down. There's always a group ready to take the mess [sic] out of anything you do."

LGBT Youth Suffer Long-Term Effects from Bullying

J.A. Muraco and S.T. Russell

J.A. Muraco and S.T. Russell are professors in the college of agriculture and life sciences at the University of Arizona.

Two new studies shed light on the long-term effect of school bullying. The first study explored the impact of bulling of LGBT [lesbian, gay, bisexual, and transgender] teens and found bullying to be related to health and adjustment differences in adulthood. The second study found that LGBT teen gender nonconformity is linked to more bullying; however, only bullying, and not teen gender nonconformity, was found to be related to well-being in adulthood. These findings highlight the long term impact bullying has on LGBT individuals.

Who Is Being Bullied, Why, and What Are the Effects?

Given the recent string of teen suicides around the country, a lot of attention has been given to school bullying. Reports indicate that up to a third of students are bullied during high school. Many schools have started programs to educate parents and students about bullying and to help students who are being bullied. One group often targeted and bullied are LGBT and gender nonconforming teens.

Although we know about immediate effects of bullying, long-term effects are still mostly unknown. A study in Finland found that having been bullied by age 8 was linked to anxiety

10–15 years later. Two studies from the United Kingdom also found negative effects of bullying for LGB adults. The first found that LGB adults who reported bullying showed higher depressive symptoms. The second found that LGB adults who reported homophobic bullying for longer periods of time at school had more stress symptoms. Of the research that has been done in the United States, none has looked at long-term effects for men and women for a range of outcomes.

Many gender nonconforming students [someone seen as having gender characteristics that are unusual] are LGBT, but not all are. Heterosexual gender nonconforming teens are likely to be bullied because others assume that they are LGBT. A growing body of research has shown that much of the bullying that takes place at school is motivated by prejudice. Bullying based on prejudice has stronger links with negative health outcomes than bullying for other reasons. Boys who are bullied by being called "gay" have greater psychological distress. Poor grades, substance use, and depression have also been linked to bullying on the basis of actual or perceived sexual orientation. Research had not, until now, explored the links between LGBT bullying, gender nonconformity, and young adult well-being.

Compared to lesbians and bisexual young women, gay and bisexual young men and transgender young adults reported higher levels of LGBT school victimization.

About the Studies

Using data from the Family Acceptance Project, Drs. Stephen T. Russell, Caitlin Ryan and colleagues were able to look at the long-term effects of LGBT teen bullying on mental and behavioral health outcomes in young adulthood. Further, they were able to explore the links between LGBT teen bullying, gender nonconformity, and young adult well-being.

The Family Acceptance Project is a community research, intervention, education, and policy program associated with San Francisco State University.

Study 1: LGBT School Bullying and the Impact on Young Adult Health and Adjustment

A total 245 LGBT young adults between the ages of 21 and 25 were surveyed. These adults answered questions about their experiences of school bullying based on their LGBT identity when they were between the ages of 13 and 19. Links between bullying, depression, suicidal ideation, life satisfaction, self-esteem, and social integration in young adulthood were then examined.

Findings show:

- Compared to lesbians and bisexual young women, gay and bisexual young men and transgender young adults reported higher levels of LGBT school victimization.

- Compared to peers who reported low levels of school victimization, LGBT young adults who reported high levels of school victimization during adolescence were:
  - 2.6 times more likely to report clinical levels of depression
  - 5.6 times more likely to report having attempted suicide
  - 5.6 times more likely to report a suicide attempt that required medical care
  - 2 times more likely to have been diagnosed with a sexually transmitted disease and to report risk for HIV infection

- Compared to peers who reported higher levels of school victimization during adolescence, LGBT young adults who reported lower levels of school victimization reported higher levels of:

- self-esteem (e.g. feeling good about themselves)
- life satisfaction (e.g. feeling good about their lives)
- social integration (e.g. feeling connected to those around them)

Study 2: Bullying, Gender Nonconformity, and Well-Being in Young Adulthood

Prior studies have shown that gender nonconforming teens are more likely to be bullied, and they are also more likely to have compromised health. Until now researchers have studied these issues separately. This study examined whether the compromised health of gender nonconforming teens could be explained by histories of bullying.

The effects of bullying, as seen in these studies, can last a decade or longer.

Young adults from the Family Acceptance Project were asked: "On a scale from 1–9, where 1 is extremely feminine and 9 is extremely masculine, how would you describe yourself when you were a teenager?" They were asked a similar question about how gender nonconforming they are now, as well as a question about how their gender conformity compares to others (from "much more feminine" to "much more masculine" on a 5-point scale). They also answered questions about their experiences of school bullying based on their actual or perceived LGBT identity when they were between the ages of 13 and 19.

Findings show:

- Although higher levels of self-reported adolescent gender nonconformity were related to more LGBT school bullying, it is school bullying, and not gender nonconformity, that most strongly predicts negative well-being in young adulthood.

Implications of the Studies

- The effects of LGBT teen bullying are serious and long lasting. The effects of bullying, as seen in these studies, can last a decade or longer. Educators need to ensure, when teaching parents and students about bullying, that they stress the impact bullying has on the lives of those being bullied.

- There are serious health disparities for LGBT adults. Decreasing LGBT bullying would likely result in significant long-term health gains and reduce health disparities for LGBT adults. Policy makers should make it a priority to ensure that all schools have anti-discrimination policies in place that protect LGBT and gender nonconforming students. Further, educators should ensure all parents and students are made aware of such policies.

- Mental health practitioners need to be aware and recognize the increased likelihood that their LGBT and gender nonconforming clients may have been bullied as teens and may still be suffering effects from that bullying. Having such an understanding from the onset can help speed-up recovery time.

Muslim Youth in California Are Targeted for Bullying

Council on American-Islamic Relations

The Council on American-Islamic Relations is a Muslim civil liberties advocacy organization.

The California chapter of the Council on American-Islamic Relation's (CAIR-CA) 2012 *Muslim Youth at School Survey* was the first statewide survey to examine the experiences of American Muslim youth at school. It targeted youth from across California and received responses from 21 counties. In total, 471 Muslim American students attending public school between the ages of 11 and 18 responded to the survey, which consisted of 10 multiple choice questions and space for comments.

Discrimination and Bullying

Through the survey, CAIR-CA sought to better understand how comfortable American Muslim students felt attending their schools and participating in the classroom. CAIR-CA also made it a goal to enhance its awareness of the extent to which students were being bullied and their responses.

California's Muslim students, for the most part, reported a healthy school environment in which they were comfortable participating in discussions about their religious identity, believed that their teachers respected their religion, and felt safe at school.

Most of the respondents came from areas of California with large and robust Muslim populations, such as Orange

County and Santa Clara County. This may account for the many responses we received from students who stated that they felt confident and supported in asserting their Muslim identity at school. While many respondents indicated that they simply internalized anti-Muslim name-calling from peers, such as "Osama Bin Laden" and "terrorist," many indicated that this did not have a long-lasting effect on them.

As evidenced by the findings in this report, there are still significant issues facing American Muslim youth at school. The majority of school-related cases reported to CAIR involve teacher discrimination. Therefore, it is significant that 18% of the surveyed students answered: 'Strongly Disagree,' 'Disagree,' or 'Undecided' when asked about feeling comfortable participating in classroom discussions and 19% of students answered: 'Strongly Disagree,' 'Disagree,' or 'Undecided' when asked if their teachers respected their religion.

As Islam and Muslims continue to be in the public spotlight, negative representations and assumptions in the public sphere serve as obstacles to cultivating a tolerant, nurturing, and healthy school environment for all students.

More than 10% of American Muslim students reported physical bullying such as slapping, kicking, or punching. Seventeen percent of the female respondents who wear a *hijab*, the Islamic headscarf, reported being bullied at least once because of this. Most importantly, 50% of American Muslim students reported being subjected to mean comments and rumors about them because of their religion. Additionally, more than 21% of students reported experiencing some form of cyberbullying.

Students had mixed reactions to reporting incidents to adults. About 63% said that they reported incidents of bullying to a teacher or principal, while only 53% said they reported to their parents. As to whether they thought reporting helped, 35% answered that it 'Never,' 'Rarely,' or 'Sometimes' helped, and only 17% answered that it 'Often,' or 'Very Often' helped.

With respect to how students reacted to their aggressors when they were bullied, 8% said that they fought back, 21% said that they insulted them back, and 11% said that they reacted by making fun of the aggressor's religion or race. Sixty-one percent reported that they never fought back, 51% said that they never insulted their aggressor, and 60% reported that they never made fun of the bully's religion or race.

School bullying is a phenonmenon that affects students from diverse backgrounds and experiences, and American Muslim students are not exempt from being subjected to harassment and discrimination at school. As Islam and Muslims continue to be in the public spotlight, negative representations and assumptions in the public sphere serve as obstacles to cultivating a tolerant, nurturing, and healthy school environment for all students.

Bullying Is Not Acceptable

CAIR-California is the oldest chapter of the Council on American-Islamic Relations, the nation's largest American Muslim civil rights and advocacy organization. Its mission is to empower American Muslims, enhance understanding of Islam, encourage dialogue, protect civil liberties, and build coalitions that promote justice and mutual understanding. CAIR-CA has nearly two decades of experience responding to issues American Muslim adults face, such as national security watch-listing and employment discrimination. CAIR is committed to serving the entire community and because of the recent focus on bullying as a national issue, our offices embarked on a statewide endeavor in 2012 to examine the experiences of American Muslim youth, which was informed by the following questions:

- What unique circumstances might American Muslim youth encounter at schools that do not affect other groups?

- To what extent are these issues affecting American Muslim youth?

- What can we do to better protect the rights of American Muslim youth at school?

As social media and technology continue to grow, so do the means to cyberbully fellow peers.

This report seeks to raise awareness, both among American Muslims and the public at large, of the complex and often difficult issues that American Muslim students face at school. Many American Muslim parents remain unaware that there are legal protections for their children, who often face problems such as bullying from peers or teacher harassment on account of religion or national origin; additionally, parents and children alike do not know that they can seek accomodation for religious practices. CAIR-CA often receives anecdotal complaints of bullying from American Muslim students, but many never formally report problems to school authorities, let alone to state and federal agencies tasked with solving these problems. This report attempts to bring these issues out of the shadows by encouraging American Muslim families to report and address bullying and harassment incidents. CAIR-CA wants American Muslim parents to know that they do not have to handle situations on their own, that schools are accountable for failure to take action, and that a decision to dismiss mistreatment and abuse as a natural consequence of being Muslim in America, or simply part of growing up, is unacceptable. . . .

How Bullying Manifests

There are four main types of bullying: physical, verbal, social/ psychological, and cyberbullying. "Physical bullying involves hurting a person's body or possessions." It can include spitting, tripping, pushing, hitting, kicking, punching, taking or damaging someone's belongings, and making offensive hand gestures. "Verbal bullying is saying or writing mean things." Verbal bullying can include name-calling, teasing, inappropriate sexual comments, and threats. "Social bullying, sometimes referred to as relational bullying, involves hurting someone's reputation or relationships." This can include spreading rumors about someone, embarrassing or excluding someone in public, or telling other children to not be friends with someone.

The fourth and most recent manifestation of bullying has transformed the phenomenon entirely. Cyberbullying is committed by means of an electronic communication device. Cyberbullying can include bullying through instant messages, text messages, and e-mails, as well as spamming or stealing a person's sensitive information. Additionally, it can include impersonation, and now, "Facebook burn pages," or Facebook pages created specifically to harass others. As social media and technology continue to grow, so do the means to cyberbully fellow peers.

While the effects of bullying can manifest differently in every child, there are universal signs parents should look out for. Physical manifestations could be cuts, bruises, or scrapes. Some psychological manifestations may take the form of anger problems, anxiety, depression, low self-esteem, and being more quiet than usual. Other indications that a child might be a target of bullying include continuously missing school, declining grades, or missing personal items like backpacks, electronic devices, or books.

American Muslims and Bias Based Bullying

While bullying can take any of the four forms previously mentioned, bullying in the context of American Muslim students is unique in that it mixes cultural and religious animosity towards Muslims with current events. The bullying can take the form of "jokes" about bombs and terrorists. Insults are often directed at students, ranging from "towelhead" to "camel jockey" to "sand n****r." Many American Muslim students regularly talk about being called a terrorist or being asked if they are related to terrorist leader Osama Bin Laden. Repeated association with negative stereotypes has been shown to cause low self-esteem and depression, developmental problems in early adolescents, and issues of identity formation. American Muslim students who choose to wear the *hijab* may have an even more difficult time because they physically wear a symbol of their faith and become easy targets for bullies. Aggressors may pull or tug on a girl's *hijab*, or will offensively touch it.

Antibullying Campaigns Ignore Sexism Against Girls and Women

Meghan Murphy

Meghan Murphy is a writer and a journalist in Vancouver, British Columbia, Canada. She is the founder and editor of Feminist Current, *Canada's most-read feminist blog; her writing has been published in* New Statesman, The Globe and Mail, The Georgia Straight, Al Jazeera, Ms. Magazine, *and numerous other venues.*

The relatively recent development of the anti-bullying campaign has been almost universally accepted as something that is unquestionably "good." These campaigns are politically correct, they are focused on kids (a largely unhateable group), and they are relatively easy to get behind for most people (with the exception of some religious groups), particularly those who consider themselves to be open-minded, liberal folks.

Bullying and Sexism

Support for these campaigns has surged in popularity with celebrity endorsements and the almost immediate, enthusiastic incorporation of anti-bullying discourse into elementary and high schools. Projects like Dan Savage's It Gets Better, aimed at inspiring hope in alienated and harassed LGBT [lesbian, gay, bisexual, and transgender] kids, are hard to criticize, particularly in light of stats around the increased likelihood of suicide attempts by these youth. But while anti-bullying campaigns grow ever more popular and schools rush to adopt anti-bullying training for teachers and parents, put on anti-bullying events and create anti-bullying programs and policies, generally patting themselves on their backs for implementing these progressive measures, the elephant in the room grows ever more visible.

That elephant is, of course, girls and women.

While incorporating words like homophobia, gender, ethnicity, or the favourite, *diversity*, into schools' plans to "tackl[e] the bullying problem," seems easy for school boards, the media, and the public to swallow, that uncomfortable word, *women*, remains distinctly absent from the conversation.

Our understanding of the ways in which young men learn to view and treat women, which begins very early on, is left, distinctly, off the table.

We seem able to talk about a number of different ways people can be bullied or harassed in schools, focusing largely on issues such as sexual orientation and gender identity, without addressing sexual harassment or without naming women and girls as a specific target. Sexism starts early. It starts in the classroom. And yet all we can manage to rally around is the neutral "bullying." Why?

Stopbullying.gov says that bullying can take many shapes and forms and isn't limited by age, gender, or education level. . . . But can it happen because of sexism? Meh. Who knows!

While we are, apparently, becoming comfortable with language around "challenging homophobic bullying" and "celebrating difference," our understanding of the ways in which young men learn to view and treat women, which begins very early on, is left, distinctly, off the table.

Bullying and Masculinity

Explaining to kids that calling someone a "fag" or using the word "gay" in a derogatory sense is happening, which is good. Part of what is missing, though, is the recognition that, generally, boys are called "gay" because they act too much "like girls." Because yes, being a girl is still a bad thing.

When [celebrity music artist] Lady Gaga got on board with anti-bullying campaigns in school, she said, as part of her message: "It is important that we push the boundaries of love and acceptance. It is important that we spread tolerance and equality for all students. . . . I am going to be working as hard as I can to make bullying a hate crime."

And sure, that's a pretty good message. Not much to argue with there. Certainly no one believes that anyone else should be harassed because they fail to conform to universal standards of masculinity (Lady Gaga, in the video, is addressing Jacques St Pierre, who "was bullied in elementary school by students who called him a fag for being interested in theatre and drama"). But let's think about what it is that it means to be a man. What it means to be masculine, as far as avoiding being called a "fag" goes, anyway. It means, not-like-a-woman. It means being tough, unemotional, often athletic (i.e. *not* into theatre) or physically strong, sometimes it means being violent or aggressive, and often, of course, we understand masculinity in terms of how a man views and treats women. In order to avoid harassment, as a boy, you must be sure to "pass" as adequately masculine. In order to be adequately masculine, you must not only be clearly not-like-a-girl, but you must see women as "less than" while simultaneously trying to f*** them. Being f***ed by a man means you are less than. As a man, if you enjoy or desire to be f***ed by another man, it means you aren't adequately masculine. And that feminization that comes along with being f***ed by men makes you deserving of harassment. This isn't, of course, the only issue at play when it comes to homophobia, but it certainly is one of them.

In light of the recent sexual harassment claims which have come out around the RCMP [Royal Canadian Mounted Police], wherein Cpl. Catherine Galliford detailed the years of harassment that eventually led her to take medical leave on account of the stress and emotional toll this treatment had taken on her, one would think a light would have gone off in someone's head.

It feels a little bit awkward to witness the immediate and eager embrace of anti-bullying campaigns while sexual harassment and sexism remain so common, so destructive, so acceptable, and yet, relatively, unaddressed.

"Hey!" One might think. "I wonder when this kind of behaviour starts?" "I wonder how men learn to treat women like sex objects?" "I wonder if there's any way we could curb this behaviour before it becomes completely normalized?"

Galliford's experience was not an anomaly. Other women have since come out about the harassment they experienced in the RCMP as well. From men planting pornography in a female co-worker's desk to propositioning to inappropriate touching, it's clear that this kind of behaviour, on the parts of men, is both common and acceptable.

But how seriously does the state take sexual harassment? And how willing are we, as a society, to actually address the issue? It feels a little bit awkward to witness the immediate and eager embrace of anti-bullying campaigns while sexual harassment and sexism remain so common, so destructive, so acceptable, and yet, relatively, unaddressed.

Address Sexual Harassment in Schools

For me, the experience of sexual harassment was introduced to me when I was about 11. I remember, very specifically, meeting with a teacher, along with several other Grade 6 girls, because the boys in our class had taken to making comments about our prepubescent (or non-existent) breasts. And while I believe the behaviour was addressed with the individual boys who were doing the harassing, there was never any kind of discussion around sexism or sexual harassment as part of any program or curriculum in all my years at school. For the rest of the boys, for those who aren't called out by individuals early on (or who don't have feminist parents), I imagine that sexual harassment just becomes part of the routine of presenting as masculine.

So I was in Grade 6 in about 1991. I imagine this kind of behaviour and sexual harassment has been experienced by many, many girls before me and continues to be a common experience today. Boys learn very early on what girls are for and they learn very early on how men *should* treat women, in order to be adequately masculine and to be accepted by their peer group.

And yet, as pointed out by a friend who is currently completing a PhD in Education, the concept of sexism and the issue of sexual harassment remains non-existent in both elementary and high school curriculums. Is it really a mystery that men grow up to sexually harass women on the streets, in the workplace, in bars, and, generally, anywhere a woman might be, when they are never taught that this behaviour won't be tolerated?

While we all seem to be madly in love with the idea of anti-bullying campaigns and have managed, very, very quickly to start creating programs across North America to address the issue of bullying in schools, we have yet, in all the years of sexism and sexual harassment (never mind rape and assault) that has existed from very early on in schools, to address the issue of patriarchy. We have yet to make a concerted effort to address the ways in which boys learn to treat women as objects that don't deserve their respect, in school. We seem to talk a lot about equality without mentioning the word sexism. We seem able to talk about gender without mentioning the word woman. And we talk a lot about harassment without mentioning the fact that both bullying and harassment are things that women experience, on a fairly constant basis, from the time they are very young. Simply because they are girls in a man's world.

When we say "gender" today, what we mean is "gender expression" or "gender identity." It has become a very neutral term and it has become a way for the state and the law to avoid naming "women" as a target. As far as anti-bullying campaigns go, girls are not named as a specific target even though "gender" and "equality" are common terms within this discourse. And while it is good that we are addressing this idea that boys need not fit into this prescribed role of "masculinity," we seem to be completely afraid to address why that is and what the consequences of a system that views masculinity as "good," simply because it isn't "femininity" are for women in that culture.

Within the neutrality of the way in which "gender" is used in anti-bullying campaigns and in the distinct absence of a focus on sexual harassment, and an absence of words like "sexism" or "patriarchy," anti-bullying campaigns appear to remain safely designated for boys.

Despite Myths, Asian Americans Are Not Disproportionately Bullied

Nellie Tran

Nellie Tran is a community psychologist and an assistant professor of counseling and school psychology at San Diego State University. She is also cochair of the Asian American Psychological Association Leadership Fellows Program.

Myth: Asian-American students are bullied far more than other ethnic groups, with 54 percent of Asian-American students reporting that they were bullied in the classroom.

Fact: Fewer Asian-American students (17 percent) reported being bullied at school than did any other ethnic groups. The 54 percent figure refers to where the bullying occurred, not the overall rate. Over half of Asian-American students who report being bullied, say its occurring in the classroom.

Myth: Asian-American students are cyberbullied far more than any other ethnic group, with 62 percent of Asian-American students reporting that they were bullied online up to twice a month.

Fact: Fewer Asian-American students (2.9 percent) reported being cyberbullied than did any other ethnic group. The 62 percent figure refers to how frequently the cyberbullying occurred among those reported being cyber-bullied, not the overall rate.

"When I was a teenager, I was bullied a lot, and I felt very insecure and very scared and I didn't want to live."—Margaret Cho [Korean-American comedian]

National Data

According to the *Indicators of School Crime and Safety: 2010* report:

- Fewer Asian-American students (18 percent) reported being bullied at school or cyberbullied than did White students (35 percent), African-American students (31 percent) or Latino students (28 percent). More Asian-American victims of bullying (11.1 percent) said that they were bullied because of their race than did White victims (2.8 percent), African-American victims (7.1 percent) or Latino victims (6.2 percent).

- Like other racial minorities, more Asian-American students (11 percent) reported being frequently targeted with race-related hate words than was reported by White students (3 percent).

Data on nearly 750 Asian American middle and high school students from the National Longitudinal Study of Adolescent Health ... suggest that 17 percent reported being violently victimized ... at least once in the past year.

Racial/ethnic minorities who break stereotypes are more likely to be bullied. Asian American and Latino student athletes were more likely to be bullied, whereas sport participation was an insulating factor for White and Black students.

Among Asian American students, immigrant and 2nd generation students were more likely to be victimized than 3rd or later generation students. Data comes from the Education Longitudinal Study of 2002 (a nation-wide sample of over 10,000 public high school students).

Data on nearly 750 Asian American middle and high school students from the National Longitudinal Study of Adolescent Health (1994–95 co-hort) suggest that 17 percent reported being violently victimized (e.g., had a gun/knife pulled on her/him, stabbed, cut or jumped) at least once in the past year.

Notable Findings from Local Studies

- Among Korean-American high school students in New York and New Jersey, 31.5 percent reported being bullied and 15.9 percent reported being aggressive victims (being bullied and bullying others). These students experienced higher levels of depression.

- A survey of more than 1,300 6th graders in California schools with predominantly Latino or Asian-American students found that Asian-Americans were the most frequently victimized ethnic group regardless of a school's racial composition.

- Asian-American, Latino and African-American students at one multiethnic public school in NYC [New York City], Asian-American students described students' verbal harassment (e.g., racial slurs, being mocked, teased) and physical victimization (e.g., being randomly slapped in hallways, physically threatened, punched, having possessions stolen) more than other racial groups.

- Chinese-American middle school students in Boston reported frequently experiencing race-based verbal and physical harassment by non-Asian peers. Harassing comments typically focused on Asian languages or accents, school performance and physical appearance. Boys more frequently reported physical harassment. Girls reported witnessing physical aggression toward Chinese-American boys.

Bullying is a form of violence that is likely widespread but under reported. According to the U.S. Department of Justice, bullying includes repeated harmful acts and a real or perceived imbalance of power between the victim and the bully:

- Bullying can be physical (assault, intimidation, destruction of property), verbal (name-calling, threats) and/or psychological/relational (could be physical or verbal; may include social exclusion, gossiping, rumors).

- Bullying can occur in person or through technology (email, chat rooms, instant messaging, text messaging or images posted on websites or sent through cellular phones).

- A person can be a bully, a victim or both (bully-victim, sometimes called aggressive victim).

Statistics and Points to Keep in Mind

- Asian-Americans are often missing or not available in nationwide data on school victimization, making it difficult to compare across groups and studies.

- How researchers ask a question determines how students will respond. Asian-American middle school boys were less likely to report being a victim when asked how often they were "bullied" in the previous month, but more boys reported being a victim when asked how often someone had repeatedly tried to hurt them or make them feel bad with specific behavior such as name-calling, threatening, shoving, spreading rumors or ignoring.

- Differences among and within Asian ethnic groups can be more important than findings across panethnic Asian-American groups. It would be useful to pay attention to findings on specific subgroups, such as Asian-American student athletes or Vietnamese-Americans, and not just those that combine all Asian-Americans into one category.

Hispanic and Immigrant Students Face Bullying

José A. Healy

José A. Healy is editions coordinator at The Wall Street Journal.

Sixteen-year-old "Feliciano" used to be called a "f--- Mexican" and pushed around by a high school classmate in Houston, Texas. He complained to his principal, his counselor and his parents, who then spoke with the other student and asked him to stop the harassment.

The bully would not listen.

Easy Targets

Tired of the verbal and physical aggression, Feliciano finally pushed back. In the confrontation, he sustained a broken arm and then obtained a court order mandating his tormenter not to come within 10 feet of him. "After the restraining order, he stopped," Feliciano recalls. "He did not bother me at all."

At five-foot-five, Feliciano feels he was singled out because of his size, dark skin and the fact that he came from a border town—easy pickings for someone 6 inches taller than he is.

Latinos at his school are the ethnic group that endures the most harassment, he says. "Every time I walk in the hallway, I see Latinos in the corner and a taller dude on them, taking money away from them."

The draw for students to look for protection by joining a *barrio* gang is as real here as it is in Mexico or Central America.

Recent immigrants are more likely to be bullied because often they have not fully adapted to mainstream U.S. customs, or they simply appear different. "In general, they become easy targets," says Sergio García, principal at Artesia High School in Lakewood, Calif., near Los Angeles. "It is a group that is not very outspoken."

Often high school and middle school students pick on immigrants—Latinos especially—for a number of reasons, including simply that they lack English-language comprehension and their awareness of U.S. customs and teen values is "different."

Unless promptly and properly addressed, friction can escalate quickly when new population groups move into settled monolithic communities lacking the capacity to serve the newcomers.

Communities newer to immigration surges can be particularly problematic, says Jerri Katzerman, director of educational advocacy at the Southern Poverty Law Center [SPLC] based in Montgomery, Alabama.

She cites public schools in Durham, North Carolina, where some teachers as well as students have told recent immigrants to "go back where they came from" or "go back to Mexico," regardless of their country of origin, according to a complaint filed by SPLC with the U.S. Department of Education's Office of Civil Rights.

Durham schools agreed this past November [2011] to take steps to protect Latino students from harassment.

New Immigrants Are Vulnerable

Unless promptly and properly addressed, friction can escalate quickly when new population groups move into settled monolithic communities lacking the capacity to serve the newcomers. Katzerman sees the conflict as "part of this entire nativist movement that is sweeping the country."

Children from rural Latin American villages arrive in garb appropriate for their home communities but fodder for ridicule on U.S. school grounds. The students wear inexpensive clothes and footwear "and end up not fitting in by today's standards," says Luis Castillo, Best Buy general manager in Alexandria, Virginia, an outspoken voice against bullying in Washington, D.C., area schools.

Those who can't afford the latest styles or technology are left out of the loop. Their "submissive" attitudes make them vulnerable, Castillo contends. Both girls and boys bring a lot of humility with them, and any child born here can look at that as a weakness.

In Southern California, with its significant population rooted in Mexico, bullying often involves second- or third-generation Mexican Americans intimidating first-generation ones.

In some "port of entry" schools, students and educators alike search for ways to confront negative behavior. At Artesia High School, García sometimes arranges meetings between the bullies and the bullied, encouraging them to put themselves in the other person's shoes to assess what is occurring. Following such dialogues, the bully often becomes the defender of the bullied, he says.

Bullying does not always pit white students against Latinos. Latinos bully Latinos, too.

Zamora recommends seeking help from trustworthy adults such as parents and counselors. He encourages showing hospitality toward students who appear different. "Just because a Latino or Chinese kid comes to our school doesn't mean we have to bully him," he says. "I treat all new arrivals as part of my family."

Ryan Zerbel, Artesia High's assistant principal, observes that second-generation immigrant students sometimes single out the struggling, more recent arrivals as tempting prey.

Latinos Bullying Latinos

Latino students—and immigrant students as a group—are often most vulnerable to being bullied and teased by their classmates. They're easy prey because of their limited English skills and lack of familiarity with teen rites of passage and U.S. customs.

However, bullying does not always pit white students against Latinos. Latinos bully Latinos, too. "It's so easy for the oppressed to become the oppressor," says Sergio García, principal at Artesia High School, situated near Los Angeles.

In New York City, the vast diversity of immigrants and ethnic groups engenders a divide and competition that triggers tensions among the many differing Latino groups and nationalities.

English teacher Chris Martínez, who taught there for two years, describes it: bullying among Puerto Ricans, Dominicans, Salvadorans and Mexican Americans occurred regularly when he taught there for two years, but it "never really turned violent."

"It was more name-calling, teasing, put-downs. I never saw anything that got physical," says Martínez. Now he teaches at Sam Houston Middle School in Garland, Texas, near Dallas, where cooperation and support among recent and past Hispanic immigrants is more the norm. He attributes the harmony to a greater appreciation for the high number of recent immigrants who live there.

"In my community, the culture is colorful. It's loud, it's lively. And the students are proud of where they come from," he says.

Fear of Schools

When it comes to Hispanic girls, Anthony Peguero, assistant professor at Virginia Tech, tells Hispanic Link that first-generation Latinas are less likely to be victims of physical attack than more assimilated Latinas. Sexual harassment is a persistent and troubling trend for all Latinas, however, Peguero says.

The Virginia Tech assistant professor adds that it's hard to track bullying statistics in the Hispanic community because students are reluctant to speak publicly on the abuses they face.

"Hispanic students by far are more likely to be afraid of the schools that they attend. They are more likely to think of their schools as unsafe or a dangerous place," he said.

Peguero attributed part of this fear on the national narrative surrounding immigration and deportations.

"Students interpret that as not trusting authority," said Peguero, who added that there was light at the tunnel for these youths: "People are now acknowledging this is a problem and this is helping people come forward." In Southern California, where a few million of its residents have roots in Mexico and Central America, bullying often consists of second- or third-generation Latinos ridiculing and intimidating the newcomers.

The degrees of discrimination and teasing across different ethnic groups and nationalities vary from region to region.

Luis Carlos Lopéz, at 24 an Arizona State University graduate who is now a correspondent in Washington, D.C., for Spanish-language *Al Día* of Philadelphia, remembers his trauma as an eight-year-old when he immigrated to San Fernando, Calif., from Nicaragua with a red shirt, a yellow Fred Flintstone's cap and two pairs of pants.

"How come the new kid doesn't change his clothes"?

A fellow student blurted that question when Luis had been there only a few weeks and to Luis's further embarrassment, the teacher informed the class that Luis came from a family of poor immigrants.

Immigrant students were routinely referred to as border-hoppers, *mojados* (wets) and in English wetbacks and mocked for their pronunciation of English words. Luis recalls vividly, "I learned English within a year. My speedy pick-up of the language wasn't based just on what I learned in class, but on the embarrassment of having other kids make fun of me."

"It's so easy for the oppressed to become the oppressor," says Artesia's García. The degrees of discrimination and teasing across different ethnic groups and nationalities vary from region to region, depending on how communities perceive immigrants and how accustomed they are to newcomers.

Jorge Gutiérrez, now a civil engineer in Phoenix, migrated from Salina Cruz, Oaxaca, Mexico, to East Los Angeles as a tenth-grader in the 1960s. He still remembers the taunts and ostracism he and a few hundred other non-English-speaking (NES) Lincoln High School students from throughout Mexico and Latin America endured. To second- and third-generation Latino classmates, they were all "TJs" (from Tijuana).

Their counselor spoke no Spanish and when the immigrant parents picketed in protest, the Mexican-American parents counter-picketed in defense of the school, which had a 50-percent dropout rate.

The phenomenon of immigrants bullying fellow immigrants has a long tradition. "We need to become united," says Artesia High Principal García. "Until we do, we are not going to be able to empower others who follow."

CHAPTER 4

How Does Bullying
Affect Older Victims?

Chapter Preface

Bullying, especially in the form of hazing rituals, can be a serious problem at fraternities on college campuses. Brooke Goldberg, writing for *MODA*, a lifestyle magazine at the University of Wisconsin-Madison (UW-Madison), reports, "Across the country, many fraternity men will say that hazing and bullying are traditions and normal protocols that come with wanting to be a brother."[1] For example, Goldberg interviewed a fraternity member at UW-Madison who reported that "males in fraternities can be asked to do dangerous activities such as chug excess amounts of water or alcohol," which can actually result in death if care is not taken.

Peter Smithhisler at *Forbes* points out that the discussion around hazing and bullying at fraternities can lead to a caricature in which all the good aspects of fraternity life are forgotten. He says that fraternities raised more than $21 million in philanthropy in 2013 and that fraternity graduation rates and grade point averages are higher than those of other undergraduates. Smithhisler argues that "when fraternities are at their best, they inspire partnership, community involvement, scholarship and leadership."[2] In order for people to appreciate the good of fraternities, he says, the excesses need to be addressed. He suggests that hazing should be eliminated altogether, and that there should be restrictions on alcohol use at fraternity events.

Sorority hazing is often less physically dangerous than fraternity hazing, but it too can lead to bullying and abuse. Lau-

---

1. Brooke Goldberg, "Bullying Within the Fraternity Scene: A Cultural Ritual or Forceful Intimidation?" *MODA*, February 14, 2014. http://modamadison.com/2014/02/14/bullying-within-the-fraternity-scene-a-cultural-ritual-or-forceful-intimidation.

2. Peter Smithhisler, "It's Time to Eliminate Hazing at College Fraternities," *Forbes*, April 7, 2014. www.forbes.com/sites/realspin/2014/04/07/its-time-to-eliminate-hazing-at-college-fraternities.

ren Paul, cofounder of the antibullying Kind Campaign, noted that in her own sorority experience "I remember so many things that happened during rush made me feel ostracized. . . . It takes you back to middle school where there is that certain 'group' mentality, people are left out and there is competition between sororities and girls."[3] Jessica Brookshire, a sorority member at Auburn University, argues that sorority hazing rituals, such as "older team members destroying the property of younger team members, forcing new members to perform embarrassing acts and subjecting them to an array of humiliation and mental torture,"[4] are no different from bullying. She adds, "In my opinion, bullying and hazing are actions born of the same intention: to feel more powerful by degrading others." Brookshire points out, however, that hazing in sororities has been eliminated, and she says that it is not, and should not be, tolerated in the sorority system.

The remainder of this chapter discusses other examples of bullying after childhood, including workplace bullying, bullying in college, and bullying in certain professions such as the military and nursing.

---

3. Quoted in Kathryn Cardin, "Bullying in College: Silent Yet Prevalent," *USA Today*, October 18, 2013. www.usatoday.com/story/news/nation/2013/10/18/college-bullying -silent-yet-prevalent/3008677.

4. Jessica Brookshire, "Bullying or Hazing," *Sorority Parents*, September 21, 2012. http:// sororityparents.com/2012/09/bullying-or-hazing-by-jessica-brookshire.

Cyberbullying Is a Problem in Universities

Vivian Luk

Vivian Luk is a reporter at the Canadian Press.

Cyberbullies have grown up.

Research out of Simon Fraser University suggests that the online abuse that has been so prevalent on the teenage battlefield is carrying through to the arena of adults at Canadian universities.

Not Just for Kids

Papers to be presented at a symposium in Vancouver on Wednesday [March 2014] say that undergraduate students are harassing their peers on social media, instructors are on the receiving end of student-led online smear campaigns, and faculty members are belittling their colleagues in emails.

"When you look at cyberbullying among younger kids, or kids in middle and high school, usually by age 15, it dies off," said education Prof. Wanda Cassidy, who worked on the study with two others.

"What was surprising was the fact that it is happening in universities to the extent that it is."

While many studies have been done on cyber abuse involving adolescents, research on the behaviour among adults is limited. Cassidy said she and her colleagues were curious to know whether teens who bully others online still do it after entering university.

The research team also wondered whether faculty staff are being targeted in cyberspace.

They surveyed over 2,000 people and interviewed 30 participants from four Canadian universities—two in British Columbia, one on the Prairies and one in Atlantic Canada.

Faculty members—mostly women—also said they've been harassed online by students or colleagues.

Though some of the data from two universities are still trickling in, the available information so far indicates roughly one in five undergraduate students has been cyberbullied, mostly through Facebook, text messages and email, Cassidy said.

Some students said they were the target of crude slurs.

"Called me a 'spoiled little rich bitch,' mocked my bulimia in public messages to others on Facebook, messaged me multiple times telling me my boyfriend was cheating on me, that I was nothing more than 'a clingy bitch, slut and loser,'" said one student who was interviewed in a focus group.

Faculty Targeted

Faculty members—mostly women—also said they've been harassed online by students or colleagues.

In one interview, a professor said she was bombarded with emails and text messages from a student who called her lousy, incompetent and useless.

"I am reporting you ... they will take away your licence, you are so stupid," the professor recalled from one message.

In another school, an instructor found herself fighting a losing battle against a colleague who was convinced she was gossiping about her.

"She texted me 73 times in one day, and over a week it was about 180 messages. When I didn't respond, it was worse," the instructor said.

Cassidy said the emergence of cyberbullying in an older population comes with grown-up consequences, such as ruined professional relationships or reputations, anxiety, sleep deprivation and thoughts of suicide.

"There was a fair proportion of people—both faculty and students—who said it made them feel suicidal . . . which is quite frightening, particularly when you think of faculty members.

"There should be some element of security that they don't have to worry about colleagues bullying them, but obviously they do feel like maybe there's no way out, there's no way getting around it."

The sense of helplessness is not uncommon, Cassidy said. The anonymity granted to cyberbullies makes it difficult to go after perpetrators.

And as more communications occur online, it becomes harder to avoid the angst that comes with reading a potentially abusive email or comment, Cassidy said.

She added that the website Rate My Professor, which allows students to grade teachers anonymously and post comments, is particularly distressing for instructors.

"Insulting and lied about me," said one professor, who claimed a student wrote defamatory remarks on the website.

Few university policies specifically address online bullying.

"I did not really feel good about going to that class knowing that someone was hating me. I almost talked about it with the class, but decided not to. It was pretty depressing and unmotivating. It was also pretty mean."

There are ways professors can combat negative comments, such as posting a video rebuttal, but for the most part, many feel there is little they can do, Cassidy said.

"You just have to forget about it and hope that it's not affecting (whether students will) take your course, or other professors are looking at it and it's your reputation."

Just over half of the surveyed students and faculty said they tried to stop cyberbullying. But less than half of them reported success. Cassidy said that's partly because few university policies specifically address online bullying.

University Policies

The research team examined 465 policies from 75 universities between November 2011 and January 2012.

One of the researchers, Simon Fraser criminology professor emerita Margaret Jackson said that many of the universities seemed dubious that online harassment in higher education should be considered cyberbullying.

"The connotation seems more applicable to younger individuals," Jackson said. "I think we've moved through that now, so there is an appreciation that if this isn't cyberbullying, it might be cyber harassment."

The study found most universities did have policies around student conduct, discrimination and harassment, but not all were specific to online venues.

Jackson said devising clear-cut policies is a good start, but universities should also put resources into counselling and prevention to reduce cyberbullying.

"I think there needs to be an appreciation on the part of faculty and students that there is an impact to their behaviour and they should be acting respectfully," Jackson said.

One of the papers resulting from the study will be published in the *Canadian Journal of Higher Education* this year [2014]. Two other papers are being peer-reviewed.

Katherine Jenkins, Louise Mensch and Lorraine Pascale Are Plagued by Sexist Cyberbullies

Jojo Moyes

Jojo Moyes writes regularly for the British daily newspaper The Telegraph *and is the author of nine novels, including* The Last Letter from Your Lover.

Only the most observant would have noticed the faint shift in classical singer Katherine Jenkins's expression as she answered a viewer's question on the television show *Something for the Weekend* last Sunday; the sudden rictus quality of her smile.

But a furious statement she posted online just after the programme ended revealed a greater drama backstage. Addressed to an unnamed online "bully," the statement read: "You've set up a false account in my name where u slate & destroy my character (sic). After blocking you, you still tried 2 find a way 2 get to me & this morning was 1 step too far. Sending in a question to be read on live TV ... to 'make me look clueless' is utterly pathetic," she wrote. Jenkins, it emerged, has been the target of this cyberstalker for over a year. "I've tried to ignore you but after this it's time to stand up to you."

Yesterday, Lynne Featherstone, the Liberal Democrat Home Office minister, unveiled proposals to introduce a specific offence of stalking, potentially also covering cyberstalking. A three-month consultation will also look at the use of restraining orders and police attitudes to stalking cases. It is a complicated issue; but it is timely. For it has been a depressing week to be female and have any kind of online presence.

On Saturday, cookery writer and presenter Lorraine Pascale posted a jaw-dropping message she had just received. It ended with the phrase: "Get off the TV c**n and know your place." (It is now in the hands of the police).

Talk to many high-profile tweeters today, and you will hear stories of extraordinary abuse directed against them.

Both she and Jenkins received a groundswell of online support. But the cyberbullying of women is becoming a matter of public concern.

Two newspaper columnists went on record last week about the online sexist abuse they suffer for the apparent sin of being female and having an opinion, while American writer Sady Doyle, weary of the level of online sexist abuse she received, has begun to document it, using the twitter hashtag: #mencallmethings. In a roundup of her unsolicited messages, reproduced on various websites yesterday, she lists, alphabetically, the abusive names she has been called in lieu of actual argument. Scanning the seemingly relentless list ('bitch' is one of the few I can repeat), the overall effect is, frankly, numbing.

One of the great joys of Twitter when it began was that it was a place where women could have an opinion, and be funny, using a public platform. Talk to many high-profile tweeters today, and you will hear stories of extraordinary abuse directed against them.

Just last week, bestselling children's author Emma Kennedy suffered her "most depressing day" on Twitter when she took issue with someone who believed he had a right to create and enjoy the image of another female celebrity with a knife through her head. Infuriated when she blocked him on Twitter, he bombarded her with aggressive emails instead.

Kennedy believes that anyone in the public eye can expect to find themselves cyberbullied now. "Quite why this is, is baffling to me. My main beef, however, is that women are treated very differently to men. Men's abuse is about their words or actions. For women, it's about their appearance and sexuality."

The urge to provoke seems to be behind much of it. You do not have to go far online to find oddballs whose sole raison d'être seems to be to get a rise out of those more successful.

But, in an age where women are increasingly judged by how they look, there seems to be increasing anger directed at those who choose to use their voice. And the downside of online access is that those who possess that anger have no filter in place to cause them to stop and think. When I interviewed a US sports writer on this topic last year, he regretted the loss of the "lick the envelope" moment of sanity that stopped many people from saying vile things.

If I spent all my time responding to every sexist comment which referred to rape and violence, I would lose my whole day. . . . You have to distinguish between a genuine cyberstalker and common or garden abuse.

Some women have chosen not to address such abuse head-on, fearful that it will inflame any cyberbullying. Indeed, Jennifer Perry, spokeswoman for the charity Network for Surviving Stalking, does not think Katherine Jenkins's decision to address her stalker online would be helpful. Ms Perry, who has advised X Factor contestants who received abuse online, said: "It's more likely to empower him that he's got her attention. She's now talking directly to him, which is what he wants."

However, the reaction of Jenkins and Pascale suggests this mood may be changing. When Tory MP Louise Mensch recently received threats to her children via email, she responded publicly: "To those who sent it; get stuffed, losers.... I don't bully easily. Or, in fact, at all." (A man was subsequently arrested in connection with the threats). Regardless of your political persuasion, it felt like an admirably punchy response.

Mensch points out that the outspoken woman has been a trope of public fascination since Dr Johnson. "But I do think it is really important for women to stand up to any perceived threat of violence, like Lorraine Pascale has done."

Mensch says that such abusive comments are now part of her working life, as they are for many female MPs. "If I spent all my time responding to every sexist comment which referred to rape and violence, I would lose my whole day, so I take a 'don't feed the trolls attitude.' You have to distinguish between a genuine cyberstalker and common or garden abuse."

Featherstone's task will be to try and make that difficult distinction. But, in the meantime, dealing with such abuse seems to have become an inevitable side effect of having any kind of profile.

Mensch is struck by the fact that many of those who commit the abuse are often "men with respectable jobs. If you confronted them, they would be deeply embarrassed. But I'd like to ask them: would your mother be happy to hear you talking to a woman like that, using gross threats of sexual violence? If you don't like her, you know what? Don't follow her. Don't read her blog. And grow up."

Workplace Bullying Is a Serious Problem

Catherine Mattice

Catherine Mattice is the president of Civility Partners LLC, a consulting firm that helps businesses overcome negative workplace behaviors.

A recent series of studies by big name job search engine CareerBuilder found that, currently, 35 percent of the American workforce feels it has been bullied on the job.

Bullying Goes Beyond High School

You may have presumed that bullying was reserved for elementary-school playgrounds and high school mean girls. But adults do indeed bully each other in the workplace. Whether a person is bullied in high school or at work, the impact is the same. The media has reported a distressing series of stories of kids and teens who have committed suicide due to peer harassment. These important stories underscore the damage bad behavior inflicts on its victims, but they stop short of highlighting the fact that bullying doesn't end on your 18th birthday.

According to DoSomething.org, students who are bullied are twice as likely to commit suicide, and one of 10 students drop out because they are bullied. According to the *Center for Excellence in School Counseling and Leadership* (CESCaL), bullied LGBT [lesbian, gay, bisexual, and transgender] students are four times more likely to attempt suicide, and they have a dropout rate three times the national average.

Similarly, according to workplace bullying researchers, 10 percent of adults who identify themselves as having been bullied think about or attempt suicide, and they call in sick to work an average of 10 more days per year than those who do not experience bullying. Adults liken workplace bullying to being beaten, physically abused, "assassinated," "maimed," "killed," "annihilated" and "raped." Adult targets experience anxiety, depression, sleepless nights, headaches, stomachaches and even Post-Traumatic Stress Disorder (PTSD).

Collect tangible evidence. Start a file with all memos, emails and documents that are aggressive.

Kinds of Adult Bullying

Adult bullying behaviors can be categorized into three sets of behaviors: Aggressive communication, humiliation and manipulation. Below are examples from my own conversations with targets:

Aggressive Communication. Two men I'll call Tom and Frank worked for a major retailer as truck drivers delivering goods from the warehouse to different stores across the country. They spent days together, and sometimes weeks, taking turns driving the truck as they moved through their designated routes. Frank constantly yelled at Tom; called him names; used foul language; and made threats like, "I'll have you fired for being so stupid." As the bullying escalated, one night Frank got in Tom's face and stuck his finger in Tom's nose to hold him in position while he yelled at him nose to nose. It all came to an end when Frank let his bullying behaviors get the best of him, and punched Tom while he was driving, causing the truck to swerve off the road. Luckily no one was injured, but the retailer and Frank were sued, and settled out of court.

Humiliation. Sarah (not her real name) was a new manager of a group of women that had been working together for 10 years. The group of women had lunch together, attended each other's family events and went on weekend trips. No doubt feeling threatened by this tight-knit group and wondering how she was ever going to be an effective manager, Sarah started with Veronica, the newest employee in the group. Sarah pointed out every mistake Veronica made, always in front of others. Sarah also told the other women that Veronica was talking badly about them behind their backs. When Veronica entered the room or passed her in the hallway, Sarah ignored the subordinate. After Veronica grew tired of Sarah and moved on to a new job, Sarah started in on Teresa. One by one Sarah removed her employees by bullying them out of the organization and replacing them with someone new. Over time, she had a new group of employees who just presumed, "That's the way it is around here."

Manipulation. Pamela, again a presumed name, worked for the same community college for 20 years. During that time she'd had five managers, all of whom had given her stellar employee evaluations and praised her work. The sixth manager, John, wasn't so complimentary or easy to work with. John's first move was to take many of Pamela's core responsibilities away from her without telling her why. He assigned new tasks with impossible deadlines—asking Pamela to produce something in three hours that would take any normal person three days. John didn't invite Pamela to staff meetings; so she was missing information about her department. After a year, John gave Pamela a performance evaluation that stated she had low quality work and deserved a pay deduction. Without providing Pamela an environment she could succeed in, her manager had set her up to fail.

How to Deal with Bullying

What can be done if you find yourself feeling bullied? Here are five tips:

1. Keep a journal of facts. This journal should be as emotion-free as possible and focus only on the actions of the bully. When incidents happen, return immediately to your

desk and write down who, what, when and where. If you'd like to keep a record of your emotions, keep a separate journal. You might eventually provide your journal of facts to HR [human resources], or even to your attorney.

2. Collect tangible evidence. Start a file with all memos, emails and documents that are aggressive.

3. Adjust your body language. When we feel attacked the options are fight or flight. Since you can't (legally, ethically or morally) punch a co-worker or run away from a conversation with your boss, your default option may be to tuck into as much of a ball as possible and hide. Don't. Focus on keeping your head up, making eye contact with the bully, pointing your toes forward, keeping both feet planted firmly on the ground, and putting your hands at your side. All of this shows you are assertive and may reduce the aggressive approach of a bully.

4. Talk to HR. When talking to HR about the bully, make the conversation about the bully. Keep the focus on the bully's behavior and make the business case for addressing the behavior. If you focus on your feelings, you may be seen as the problem and might not find the help you're looking for.

5. Know you may not win this battle. At some point, if the organization won't help, ask yourself how much your life and your dignity is worth. I bet it's worth more than what you're being paid. If you're not getting the help you need from HR, the tough reality may be that you need to find a new job.

The good news, even in a tough job market, is that you might become happier and less susceptible to the bullying simply by beginning your job search.

Teachers Face Bullying and Hostile Workplaces

Katie Osgood

Katie Osgood is a special education teacher at a psychiatric hospital in Chicago. Before that, she taught in the Chicago public school system and in Japan.

Recently, in Chicagoland, a story hit the papers about a teacher committing suicide. She wrote in her suicide note that the major reason for this drastic act was work-related. According to her colleagues, this woman took her own life because of the bullying and fear she experienced at her school.

Teaching Is Stressful and Abusive

As I discussed this event with a friend who is a current CPS [Chicago Public Schools] teacher, he mentioned that in the comments section of the article many non-educators were shocked and horrified at this tragic happening but were also quick to assume that the woman must have been "soft" or had some kind of underlying mental health problem. But, he quipped, when many CPS teachers heard about the incident, they just shook their heads and said, "Yeah, I can see that happening."

Truth is, so could I. When I think back to my measly one year of teaching at a horribly-run CPS elementary school, I can very easily imagine that scenario unfolding with a number of my colleagues and yes, even with myself.

Did you all catch that? Suicide is not considered shocking in the realm of teaching in CPS.

And I don't think the general public understands the toll that years of working in an increasingly horrible environment coupled with the latest wave of teacher-bashing actually takes on the people who do the hard work of education.

Let me try and paint you a picture:

Imagine you've had one of the worst weeks of your life. You haven't slept in months, you have money troubles building, your relationships are failing, you feel unheard and unappreciated at home and at work, you worry daily about your future and whether or not you will have a job next year or even next week, and the idea of getting up to go to work the next day is practically unbearable. You need a moment to catch your breath, a moment to clear the clutter of worry, failure and fear from your clouded mind. But you don't get it. There is too much to get done. And all the while, you think, if I don't get it done, I am failing these kids. I have no choice but to keep pushing.

Now add onto that a vindictive, power-hungry boss who would fire you as soon as look at you, and colleagues at work who are themselves so tired, afraid and overwhelmed that they are one bad day from breakdown.

The great irony is that as the powers that be complain about "quality" teachers they create teaching environments where it becomes impossible to be great.

And then there are your students. God you love them. But some of them have problems you simply do not know how to fix. Or, even with the interventions you know to do through experience and training, you also know it will take all of your mental energy to implement them. You don't have that kind of energy left. Some of your kids are currently homeless and show up to school unbathed and with dirty clothes. Others have developed significant behavior problems and despite your best efforts, they continue to fight, curse, and act out in class. Some of them are so embarrassed they can't read that they throw books off their desks and rip up their hand-outs.

You know deep down that most of the difficulties your children face are beyond your control. But still, most days you come home and cry because of the guilt and helplessness.

Testing and Blame

You also know that your job is on the line if you don't get these kids to perform on some silly test. You know the tests are a joke, that they do not capture the intelligence, wit, humor and spark that live within your students. But still they hang there, always lurking in the shadows. Time is slowly marching until the day you must administer the dreaded test and seal your fate.

Now imagine turning on your TV or flipping through the *Tribune* or *Sun-Times* to see yet another story loudly proclaiming that the problem with America's schools is, well, you. "More teachers must be fired!" they scream. "Teachers are the ones failing the kids, we need to hold them accountable!" "Teachers are lazy and need to work longer, harder, for less pay!" "Teacher pensions are destroying our economy!" (Whoa, did I miss the part where newspapers yelled at the people who caused the financial crisis that is slashing education budgets around the country? Are the mortgage brokers, big banks and financial industries getting demeaned every five seconds? How about the corporations not paying their fair share of taxes which help schools? And don't forget the politicians and their horrible education policies. Surely no one reading the news is believing this baloney, are they?) And every time you hear the insults or name-calling you think to yourself, "Well what the heck are any of *you* doing to help these kids. . . ." The unfairness of it all burns.

Now stretch that one terrible week into nine months. Welcome to CPS.

Of course, the great irony is that as the powers that be complain about "quality" teachers they create teaching environments where it becomes impossible to *be* great. Teachers at my old school started to look like the walking dead as the stress and fear accumulated. The increased "accountability" robbed us all of the very qualities which would make us great teachers: our passion, kindness, drive, energy, camaraderie and humor.

And then there are people, like our lovely mayor [Rahm Emanuel], who seem to enjoy kicking you while you're down. Rahm would have us believe that something like extending the school day is so easy. Oh, that smirk on his face as he seems to say "How dare you expect to be *paid* for your extra time!" And "Sure, you've been working this whole year close to break-down, barely scraping by, without any resources and with abnormally large class sizes, but I'm sure you can come up with 90 extra minutes of activities for your kids. Oh, and if you really cared, you'd do this willingly and for free. And stop asking for paper to make copies or books for them to read, you greedy teachers. And no, we are not going to fix your school building, give you the resources you say you need, or help you in any way, shape, or form. You suck, your school sucks, and we are just biding our time until we can shut the whole thing down."

Sigh. . . .

Compassion Fatigue

Now, maybe not every school and every teacher has as bad a time as that, but I know I did. And I know too many other teachers out there who are experiencing that same fear, intimidation, and stress. Teaching under these unacceptable conditions has become the rule, not the exception. I recently came across a blog post which described something called "compassion fatigue" which is "a combination of physical, emotional, and spiritual depletion associated with caring for patients in significant emotional pain and physical distress." The author goes on to say:

Like nurses, teachers confronting these pathologies [such as abuse, abandonment and alienation] are forced to perform triage. But teachers still have to somehow find the time and energy afterward to teach the subject matter they were hired to do. The debilitating effects on them are cumulative. It's little wonder, therefore, that teachers in inner-city schools have a higher rate of absenteeism and turnover than their colleagues in the suburbs. It's also not at all surprising that teachers who are faced with the challenge often find themselves drawing away from their students. The same sadness and despair that nurses report also affect teachers.

Remember, fighting for teachers is fighting for students.

Now, if you've been paying attention to the education reform debate at all in recent years, you will know that this is the place in the story where the corporate reformers of the nation, you know, the Michelle Rhees, Bill Gates, Arne Duncans,[1] and yes, Rahm Emanuels, would jump in and say something ridiculous like "no excuses" or "poverty is not destiny." They will fill your ear with talk of "the soft bigotry of low expectations" while completely ignoring the hard bigotry of poverty, racism and crippling income inequality. Their ignorance of the reality of life for students and teachers alike in the inner cities is frankly, criminal.

No more I say.

Fight Back

This post is for all my teacher colleagues out there. It's time for us to fight back. It's time to take back our profession. Teachers, use your natural inclination to educate and start teaching your friends and families about the hard realities of

---

1. Michelle Rhees was chancellor of the Washington, DC, school system from 2007 to 2010; Bill Gates is a philanthropist who has been involved in education reform; and Arne Duncan is US Secretary of Education.

our profession. And don't be afraid to sing our praises. What we do is good work and it needs to be protected and cherished.

And while you're at it, don't forget to teach as many people as possible about the true nature of corporate reform and how it's left behind entire neighborhoods. Let people know about the ridiculous goals of No Child Left Beind, and the evils behind high-stakes testing. Tell the truth about charters, that they are not, in fact, miracles. Speak up about the reality of Teach for America—how placing untrained novices in classrooms with the hardest to educate students is unjust and wrong. Make people start to at least question the hype!

More than anything, make the act of teacher-bashing unacceptable. We know that when we are overwhelmed, upset, fatigued, demoralized and stressed out beyond our limits, we will be no good for our students. Remember, fighting for teachers *is* fighting for students.

So fight for the kinds of teaching environments which benefit kids. Fight for workplaces where teachers do not flee, breakdown, or God forbid take their own lives. Fight for a steady and strong group of committed professionals who actually stick around long enough to bring the slow change that is needed in our schools. Fight for the respect we deserve. Fight for the autonomy to make decisions on curriculum, implementation, and assessment that help the kids sitting in front of us. Fight for equity in resources so we have the tools to acutally do the difficult job of teaching. Fight for the mental health that we need to be the excellent educators kids deserve.

By fighting, we can beat back some of the hopelessness and exhaustion. We need to stop blaming ourselves, alone and guilty, and instead get angry at the forces that are hurting us and the important work we do. And all you non-educators out there need to get angry right alongside us.

NFL Bullies

Emily Bazelon and Josh Levin

Emily Bazelon is a Slate *senior editor, the Truman Capote Fellow for Creative Writing and Law at Yale Law School, and the author of* Sticks and Stones: Defeating the Culture of Bullying and Rediscovering the Power of Character and Empathy. *Josh Levin is* Slate's *executive editor.*

Richie Incognito [of the Miami Dolphins football team] has been a force of destruction in the NFL [National Football League] for years. Not the football-blessed, blocking-and-tackling kind of destruction—the raging, you-would've-been-fired-500-times-if-you-weren't-a-football-player kind. This is a player who has been practically begging for the authorities to come down on him hard. In his career with the [St. Louis] Rams, [Buffalo] Bills, and [Miami] Dolphins, Incognito has drawn an enormous number of fines and penalties for his on-field behavior, and won the wrong kind of acclamation from his peers as the league's dirtiest player. Instead of punishing him, the NFL let him keep playing and messing with other people—officials, fans, opposing teams. When one team dropped him, another picked him up. His current employer, the Dolphins, has even traded on his hell-raising persona, dressing him up as a croquet player in a cheeky video on appropriate fan behavior.

Now, the offensive lineman has been suspended for conduct detrimental to his team. The surprising reason: He's been accused of bullying a teammate. At more than 300 pounds, Jonathan Martin doesn't seem like a victim out of central casting. Indeed, when reports surfaced over the weekend [November 2013], with pretty compelling examples of how Incognito had poisoned the Dolphins' locker room, the team's first response was to dismiss "the notion of bullying" as "based on speculation."

On Sunday, the team quickly reversed its position, perhaps due to the unveiling of threatening, racial-slur-laden text messages and voice mails sent from Incognito to Martin. The speedy shift is a testament to the awfulness of Incognito's alleged deeds and to the power of the word *bullying* in this cultural moment. This episode represents a test of NFL culture. After years of rising awareness about the harm bullying does kids, is football ready to appreciate the harm of letting an adult bully run rampant? Will the NFL quit pretending that it's OK to humor a poisonous misanthrope like Incognito as long as he performs on the field?

In every NFL locker room, older players take advantage of younger ones, sticking them with huge dinner bills and making them carry the veterans' pads.

In the first press reports, Martin sounded like the problem, at least from football's point of view. ESPN.com, like the Dolphins organization, initially downplayed the issue by saying he'd been the "subject of some ribbing" and was receiving professional assistance for emotional issues. The implication was that if Martin couldn't hack it in the Dophins locker room, he was the one who needed help.

Supporting the Bully

But as more details have emerged, the narrative has shifted. In addition to those horrible voice mails and texts, it's been revealed that teammates called Martin "Big Weirdo," that they stood up when he tried to sit with them at lunch, and that Martin felt pressured to pay $15,000 towards the offensive line's trip to Las Vegas, an outing he didn't even attend. CBS

Sports' Jason La Canfora reported that "Incognito has had to be reprimanded in the past for his actions toward team employees. . . . It is not uncommon for him to intentionally walk into people and make others feel uncomfortable." In a clip from HBO's documentary series *Hard Knocks,* you can see Incognito's bullying behavior for yourself. The offensive lineman steals rookie Michael Egnew's iPad and posts demeaning messages on his Facebook account—a "prank" that's very jerky and not particularly funny.

The power dynamic here is obvious. Incognito, the long-tenured player, has license to haze his teammate because he's a callow newcomer. In every NFL locker room, older players take advantage of younger ones, sticking them with huge dinner bills and making them carry the veterans' pads. This behavior is sanctioned—or at the very least not at all discouraged—by the league and by teams, and it gets passed on from generation to generation. Guys who've been bullied as rookies turn around and bully the next group. "I felt like those are the things you have to do in order to be a part of the team," the [Dallas] Cowboys' Dez Bryant said when, as a rookie, he was hit with a mindboggling $54,896 dinner tab. "The older guys helped me understand that everybody goes through it. It happened. It's no big deal. Everything's fine. Everybody is having fun. That's the great thing about it." Yes, sounds great, Dez!

The NFL, it seems, does a much better job providing a supportive, nurturing environment for someone like Richie Incognito than it does for players like Jonathan Martin.

The line between light-hearted ribbing and malicious attacks is often fuzzy. Based on the reports we've been seeing about the Dolphins' locker room, and the domineering role Incognito played inside it, there's no fuzziness here.

Incognito, it seems, has spent his life training for the role of locker-room villain. It would take too long to recount all of his alleged on-field and off-field misdeeds, but here's a brief sketch. As an undergrad at [University of] Nebraska he was ejected from a game for fighting and was spotted spitting on another player. (Years later, an NFL player would also accuse Incognito of spitting in his face.) Off the field, he was found guilty of a misdemeanor assault charge, and eventually left the Nebraska team after being indefinitely suspended for violations of team rules. With his first NFL team, the Rams, he was once fined $25,000 for berating an official. The Rams cut him in 2009 when he head-butted two opponents in the same game, drawing two 15-yard penalties and $50,000 in fines. In recent years, the [Houston] Texans' Antonio Smith accused Incognito of trying to break his ankle, then became so incensed at the Dolphins player this preseason that he ripped Incognito's helmet off and swung it at him. And this August [2013], Incognito was reported to have punched a security guard, though he was never charged or arrested. NFL.com recently did a big, splashy feature, showcasing Incognito as a guy who'd conquered his inner demons. In the piece, by Jeff Darlington, he confessed to "partying every night" when he was with the Rams, drinking and doing drugs. Darlington wrote Incognito was now taking the medication Paxil, and that he'd taken up meditation. He also noted that Incognito was bullied as a child due to his large size, and quoted Incognito's father's advice to his son: "You don't take no s--- from anyone. If you let anyone give you s--- now, you're going to take s--- your entire life."

Changing the Culture

Richie Incognito is a cautionary tale. He has problems with anger, he was bullied himself, and he was urged to fight by those closest to him. (When it comes to modeling appropriate behavior, Incognito's dad does not seem to be doing a great job. On Monday morning, *Deadspin* presented compelling evidence that Richie Incognito Sr. was writing horrible, anonymous attacks on Jonathan Martin on online message boards.) And though there were a few bumps along the way, his behavior has mostly been encouraged and rewarded with fame and big-money contracts. The Rams only cut Incognito after his head-butts hurt them on the field, costing the team two 15-yard penalties. Otherwise, they seemed willing to keep on excusing his lapses of judgment, saying "he understands that it can't happen again."

The NFL, it seems, does a much better job providing a supportive, nurturing environment for someone like Richie Incognito than it does for players like Jonathan Martin. Suspending Incognito for his locker-room bullying could stop that cycle. It could also lead to a change in how the NFL deals with people like Incognito, who probably need counseling more than they do coaching, and with victims like Martin. If Martin gets the NFL and his team's support for talking honestly about the culture of the Dolphins' locker room, that would go a long way toward airing the damage teams can do when they turn on one of their own. It was amazing on Sunday to see ex-players like Ray Lewis and Shannon Sharpe talk seriously about the problem of interpersonal team dynamics, and when locker-room bullying can go too far. Hopefully it won't just be a one-day conversation.

And if the NFL can switch from enabling its Incognitos to helping its Martins, the latter player could become a modern-day Rosey Grier. Back in the 1970s, Grier—an all-pro defensive lineman—performed the song "It's Alright to Cry" on the album *Free To Be You and Me*. In the cities and towns where football is king, an NFL player copping to human vulnerability can truly make it easier for kids to do the same thing.

Bullying Is a Problem in Police Academies

David C. Couper

David C. Couper was the chief of police of Madison, Wisconsin, for twenty years.

Last week I read an article in the *New York Times Magazine* about police training in Atlanta. It reminded me of my days in the Marines—not my 33 years in the police.

Police Officers Are Not Soldiers

I spent a decade on active and reserve duty as a U.S. Marine. I was an enlisted man and went through a tough 12-week boot camp in San Diego in the late 1950s. The things I was asked to do and bear made sense given my chosen occupation: I was to be a fighting man—to seek out, engage, and destroy an enemy.

When I left the Marines and set off to become a police officer, I thankfully was trained as a police officer and not a soldier. That made sense to me as I quickly understood that there was a big difference between the two.

Now back to the *Times* story: it was about Jacob Mach's journey to America from the Sudan. He was one of the 4,000 "Lost Boys" of the Sudan. After coming to America 12 years ago, he now was training to become an Atlanta police officer. . . .

What I saw in this documentary was a questionable learning environment that both emotionally and physically stressed its students.

During my years as a police leader, I tried to teach other police departments the best way to go about preparing young men and women to become police officers. This was not one of them.

Is it necessary to bully and abuse police recruits in order to teach them the skills necessary to be an effective police officer today?

Bullying as Training

I stress in my book *Arrested Development: A Veteran Police Chief Sounds Off About Protest, Racism, Corruption, and the Seven Steps Necessary to Improve our Nations' Police* that police officers need to be college educated, well-trained, controlled in their use of force, honest, and respectful. The following is a story about one of my experiences teaching leadership and improvement methods to a large urban police department in the West:

> As I was setting up my classroom at their training academy, I looked out the window and observed a formation of their new police recruits. I decided to go outside and get a closer look. The recruits were standing in three ranks—it was an inspection, a situation I could easily relate to from my days as a Marine.
>
> Suddenly, the training instructors started yelling at the new officers. Some were ordered to do push-ups by way of the familiar military command: "Drop and give me ten." In addition, I heard the instructors calling the young officers "assholes." I returned to the classroom in time to greet the chief and his command staff. I introduced myself and the curriculum for the next three days, then asked, "Are your officers permitted to call citizens names?" They seem shocked. "We have rules against doing that. Why do you ask?"

"Well," I replied, "I was watching your new officers outside this window and observed your trainers calling them very derogatory names. You know, it really doesn't matter if you have rules against such conduct because when their teachers call them names, they will think that it's okay for them to do the same to citizens. And if you ever try to discipline them, their defense will simply be, 'That's what the department taught me.'"

I recently learned that the department never did change. Their academy remains stress-based, military, and intimidating. I don't know if their training officers ever stopped calling recruit officers names. But one thing I do know, is that if they don't stop, I predict they will continue to have problems with officers disrespecting citizens. How could they expect any different kind of an outcome?. . .

Half of our nation's police academies train in an atmosphere police trainers themselves identify as stress-based; that is, intimidating, even bullying. This makes half of American police academies more like military boot camps or correctional facilities than places in which college-educated young men and women are prepared to be professional police practitioners. . . .

Today, many police departments still continue to run their training academies like boot camps. These departments have training officers who look and act like Marine Corps drill instructors. They even wear the familiar Smoky Bear hats of a Marine drill instructor. As I became more acquainted with police work, I couldn't understand why police were using the same training model I had been subjected to as a Marine. There was no similarity whatsoever between being a Marine infantryman and a police officer—the two job functions were as different as night and day.

Hazing Teaches Nothing

I found this documentary about police training in Atlanta to be very unsettling. I challenge the basic assumptions about the efficacy of this model. First of all, is it necessary to bully and abuse police recruits in order to teach them the skills necessary to be an effective police officer today? Do people learn better under encouragement than stress? I think we all know the answer.

This kind of debasing treatment in one way or another continues as the primary training protocol in at least half of our nation's police training academies. It must stop.

Secondly, if the stress-based, boot camp style is a necessary part of police work, why aren't the highly-valued physical fitness requirements required of all police officers during their careers, not just at the beginning? (In fact, the only skill that continues to be evaluated by most police departments is periodic firearms, and not physical fitness, qualification standards.)

The best argument against this method of teaching occurs in the documentary itself. It was when Mach was having trouble on the shooting range and we see two styles of teaching used on him: one by an aggressive and demeaning male instructor and the other by a nurturing female instructor. Which one was effective in helping Mach qualify that day? Of course, the instructor who acted in a helping and humane manner.

This kind of debasing treatment in one way or another continues as the primary training protocol in at least half of our nation's police training academies. It must stop.

At the end of the documentary, Mach was dismissed from the academy. Thankfully, he found a job as an Atlanta city Code Enforcement Officer. Watching him work effectively in this new job tells me that given another kind of training environment he would be a successful police officer.

The other thing that troubles me is that while we, as a nation, are working to eliminate hazing and bullying in our nation's schools and workplaces, we need to take a better look at how our recruit police officers are treated. Hazing and bullying does not teach anyone anything except how to haze and bully. And they are not the kind of things we want our nation's police to know let alone be subjected to.

Bullying Is a Problem
in the Military

Margaret Carlson

Margaret Carlson is a Bloomberg View columnist and a former White House correspondent for Time.

The U.S. Army seems determined to get it right this time.

Instead of lying, as the brass did in the 2004 death of Pat Tillman in Afghanistan, the military owned up to the awful truth that a 19-year-old private, Danny Chen, died at the hands of his fellow soldiers. Unlike the celebrated professional football player, Chen didn't fall in a hail of friendly fire in a raid gone horribly wrong but, according to the Army, alone in a guard tower in Kandahar Province from a single bullet to the head.

In Tillman's case, a fantasy was crafted by General Stanley McChrystal and the White House to make him a hero, at least until they got through his televised memorial service. Their mistake was to assume that Tillman's family would stand for the lie. They didn't. They fought until the truth came out.

Chen's parents, however, don't have the resources of the Tillmans. Neither speaks English, and both work in New York's Chinatown, his mother as a seamstress, his father as a cook. They've relied on a neighborhood community organization to help them deal with the death of their only child.

Their modest circumstances make it all the more noteworthy that the Defense Department didn't try to whitewash the tragedy. Within three months of the death of the Chens' only child, the Army came back with charges, including manslaughter and negligent homicide, against eight soldiers in his unit.

Pelted with Rocks

What the family has learned so far is chilling: Hours before Chen's death, his comrades in arms, who'd presumably protect him to the death in a foxhole, instead dragged him out of bed, forced him to crawl on the ground as they pelted him with rocks and made him do pull-ups while holding water in his mouth. All this, his tormentors say, because Chen had failed to turn off the heater in the shower.

> *It's not such a surprise that bullying goes unreported. Yet the military knows there are terrible psychological problems ravaging the ranks.*

Yet the Chens are shocked by the Army's initial conclusion that their son took his own life. Although in letters home he complained that he'd run out of ways to deal with the ridicule—there are few Asians in the military, and he was frequently taunted—he didn't seem depressed.

The Army should be commended for not stonewalling. Yet how is it possible that Chen could have been so abused without anyone in authority knowing of his torment, in a place where military discipline is enforced and where eyes are open 24/7?

I understand the silence. My brother, who suffered seizures at birth that left him brain-damaged, was fair game in the neighborhood. He couldn't read, write, get a joke or learn how to grip a bat. Many times, I would fight the kids who picked on him and insist he be selected for a team. Other times, I wanted to be part of the group and abandoned him. He would stand around kicking holes in the dirt until it was time to go home. I never told my mother. Neither did he.

We were both too ashamed, so it's not such a surprise that bullying goes unreported. Yet the military knows there are terrible psychological problems ravaging the ranks. The high suicide rate is one indication. According to a report from the Center for a New American Security, a member of the armed forces committed suicide every 36 hours between 2005 and 2010; the report released in October [2011] shows that there were a record 33 suicides of active and reserve personnel serving in the Army in July of this year.

No one can ever know what pushes someone over the line, but bullying, said Eugene Fidell, the former president of the National Institute of Military Justice, is a recurring problem, especially in a closed environment filled with the young and vulnerable. "Can I imagine somebody being bullied in the military to the point of taking his or her own life? Yes," Fidell said.

Zero Tolerance

At a news conference Dec. 21 [2011], Captain John Kirby, a Pentagon spokesman, said there is a zero-tolerance policy toward what he euphemistically called hazing. Nonetheless, he recognized that it "occasionally occurred." Defense Secretary Leon Panetta said last week that the issue has his "personal attention" and ordered military commanders to review anti-bullying policies.

In 2010, two Army sergeants were imprisoned for three to six months and one other was given a reduction in pay after a private, Keiffer Wilhelm, killed himself 10 days after arriving in Iraq. His family said he was forced to run for miles with rocks in his pockets. In October, several Marines were court-martialed for the death of an Asian-American who killed himself in April after what prosecutors called hazing.

Senator Kirsten Gillibrand, a New York Democrat who serves on the Armed Services Committee, said Chen's death is a symptom of a larger problem and last week she called on the Defense Department to conduct a systemwide review of hazing.

As they should. It's hard to know what's more senseless, the killing of Tillman by friendly fire or the killing of Chen by unfriendly fire.

One of the eight soldiers charged in Chen's death is an officer. First Lieutenant Daniel J. Schwartz. So far, he's been charged only with dereliction of duty, even though he was the one who could have stopped Chen's ordeal.

Had one of the kids' parents been in the park and joined in the abuse of my brother, that wouldn't be called dereliction of duty. It would be called criminal.

Organizations to Contact

The editors have compiled the following list of organizations concerned with the issues debated in this book. The descriptions are derived from materials provided by the organizations. All have publications or information available for interested readers. The list was compiled on the date of publication of the present volume; names, addresses, phone and fax numbers, and e-mail and Internet addresses may change. Be aware that many organizations take several weeks or longer to respond to inquiries, so allow as much time as possible.

American Civil Liberties Union (ACLU)
125 Broad St., 18th Floor, New York, NY   10004
(212) 549-2500
website: www.aclu.org

The American Civil Liberties Union is a national organization that works to defend Americans' civil rights as guaranteed in the US Constitution. The organization publishes the semiannual newsletter *Civil Liberties Alert.* Its website includes congressional testimony and briefing papers such as "Free Speech and Cyber-bullying."

American Psychological Association (APA)
750 First St. NE, Washington, DC   20002-4242
(202) 336-5500
e-mail: public.affairs@apa.org
website: www.apa.org

The American Psychological Association is the primary scientific and professional psychology organization in the United States. Its official position is that all forms of bullying exert short- and long-term harmful psychological effects on both bullies and their victims. Its available resources include the "APA Resolution on Bullying Among Children and Youth." The APA's website offers links to a research roundup, bullying prevention programs around the world, and a "Getting Help" section for adolescents and adults dealing with bullying issues.

American School Counselor Association (ASCA)

1101 King St., Suite 625, Alexandria, VA   22314

(703) 683-2722 • fax: (703) 683-1619

e-mail: asca@schoolcounselor.org

website: www.schoolcounselor.org

The American School Counselor Association sponsors workshops such as "Bullying and What to Do About It" and publishes the bimonthly magazine *ASCA School Counselor*. Free online resources include the articles "The Buzz on Bullying" and "Appropriate Use of the Internet." The ASCA's online bookstore offers titles aimed at young people, such as *Cool, Calm, and Confident: A Workbook to Help Kids Learn Assertiveness Skills*; antibullying posters, banners, and bulletin boards; and sample lesson plans for school-based antibullying programs.

Gay, Lesbian, and Straight Education Network (GLSEN)

90 Broad St., 2nd Floor, New York, NY   10004

(212) 727-0135

e-mail: glsen@glsen.org

website: www.glsen.org

Founded in 1990, the Gay, Lesbian, and Straight Education Network fosters a healthy and safe school environment where every student is respected regardless of sexual orientation. It is the oversight organization of more than four thousand school-based Gay-Straight Alliances and the sponsor of two antidiscrimination school events, the National Day of Silence and No Name-Calling Week. Its antibullying initiatives include the educational website ThinkB4YouSpeak.com and the monthly e-newsletter *Respect Report*. The GLSEN website offers research reports such as *From Teasing to Torment: School Climate in America; A National Report on School Bullying* and *Shared Differences: The Experiences of Lesbian, Gay, Bisexual and Transgender Students of Color*; and an antibullying toolkit called the New Safe Space Kit.

Girlshealth.gov
Office on Women's Health
US Department of Health and Human Services
200 Independence Ave. SW, Room 712E
Washington, DC   20201
website: www.girlshealth.gov

Girlshealth.gov is a website maintained by the Office on Women's Health within the US Department of Health and Human Services. Its purpose is to provide reliable and accurate information on health issues specific to young women. Topics on the site include bullying, body, drugs, alcohol, smoking, and relationships. With regard to bullying, the website discusses cyberbullying, the unique ways that girls experience bullying, and how girls can address bullying themselves.

Great Schools
160 Spear St., Suite 1020, San Francisco, CA   94105
website: www.greatschools.org

Great Schools works to provide information about schools' performance across the country with the hope of providing parents with the necessary details to choose the appropriate schools for their children. The organization also focuses on many school-related issues, including bullying. Articles such as "Bullying: What You Can Do," "How They Do It in Finland," and "Don't Just Stand There" can all be accessed on the organization's website.

International Bullying Prevention Association (IBPA)
PO Box 99217, Troy, MI   28099
(800) 929-0397
e-mail: info@ibpaworld.org
website: www.ibpaworld.org

The International Bullying Prevention Association is an international organization dedicated to promoting bullying prevention and policies based on sound research to create safer schools, improve work environments, and advance society.

IBPA sponsors conferences to foster discussion about the problem of bullying and provides resources on its website for educators, parents, teens, and kids. These resources link to Stopbullying.gov and offer each of these group's suggestions on ways to get involved and stop bullying.

National Bullying Prevention Center

PACER Center, 8161 Normandale Blvd.
Bloomington, MN 55437
(888) 248-0822 • fax: (952) 838-0199
e-mail: bullying411@pacer.org
website: www.pacer.org/bullying

Funded by the US Department of Education's Office of Special Education Programs, the National Bullying Prevention Center is an advocate for children with disabilities and all children subject to bullying, from elementary through high school. Bullying and cyberbullying prevention resources (available in English, Spanish, Hmong, and Somali) include audio-video clips, reading lists, creative writing exercises, group activities, and numerous downloadable handouts such as "Bullying Fast Facts." The center sponsors school and community workshops and events such as National Bullying Awareness Week each October.

National Crime Prevention Council (NCPC)

2001 Jefferson Davis Hwy., Suite 901, Arlington, VA 22202
(202) 466-6272 • fax: (202) 296-1356
website: www.ncpc.org/cyberbullying

The National Crime Prevention Council was founded in 1979 to get citizens, especially youth, involved in crime prevention. The council's cyberbullying campaign includes a public service ad contest (winning ads can be viewed on the website), free antibullying banners users can copy and paste into e-mail or social networking pages, the Be Safe and Sound in School program, and educational training manuals to help youth and adults manage bullying and intimidation. Downloadable resources include a range of podcasts and research papers such as the Harris Interactive report, *Teens and Cyberbullying*.

Olweus Bullying Prevention Program
Institute on Family and Neighborhood Life
Clemson University, 158 Pool Agricultural Center
Clemson, SC   29634-0132
(864) 710-4562 • fax: (406) 862-8971
e-mail: nobully@clemson.edu
website: www.clemson.edu/olweus

Developed by Norwegian bullying researcher Dan Olweus in the 1980s, the Olweus Bullying Prevention Program is a school-based intervention program designed to prevent or reduce bullying in elementary, middle, and junior high schools (students six to fifteen years old). It is endorsed as a model antibullying program by the US Substance Abuse and Mental Health Services Administration and by the Office of Juvenile Justice and Delinquency Prevention. The website includes information on how the program works, on statistical outcomes, and on studies of the effectiveness of this and other antibullying programs.

Bibliography

Books

Michelle Anthony and Reyna Lindert — *Little Girls Can Be Mean: Four Steps to Bully Proof Girls in the Early Grades*. New York: St. Martin's Griffin, 2010.

Jed Baker — *No More Victims: Protecting Those with Autism from Cyber Bullying, Internet Predators, and Scams*. Arlington, TX: Future Horizons, 2013.

Emily Bazelon — *Sticks and Stones: Defeating the Culture of Bullying and Rediscovering the Power of Character and Empathy*. New York: Random House, 2013.

danah boyd — *It's Complicated: The Social Lives of Networked Teens*. New Haven, CT: Yale University Press, 2014.

Barbara Coloroso — *The Bully, the Bullied, and the Bystander: From Preschool to High School—How Parents and Teachers Can Help Break the Cycle*. New York: HarperCollins, 2010.

Maureen Duffy and Len Sperry — *Overcoming Mobbing: A Recovery Guide for Workplace Aggression and Bullying*. New York: Oxford University Press, 2014.

Peter Goldblum et al., eds. | *Youth Suicide and Bullying: Challenges and Strategies for Prevention and Intervention.* New York: Oxford University Press, 2014.

Thomas A. Jacobs | *Teen Cyberbullying Investigated: Where Do Your Rights End and Consequences Begin?* Minneapolis, MN: Free Spirit Publishing, 2010.

Robin M. Kowalski, Susan P. Limber, and Patricia W. Agatston | *Cyberbullying: Bullying in the Digital Age,* 2nd ed. Hoboken, NJ: Wiley-Blackwell, 2012.

Butch Losey | *Bullying, Suicide, and Homicide: Understanding, Assessing, and Preventing Threats to Self and Others for Victims of Bullying.* New York: Routledge, 2011.

Pamela Lutgen-Sandvik | *Adult Bullying: A Nasty Piece of Work—Translating a Decade of Research on Non-Sexual Harassment, Psychological Terror, Mobbing and Emotional Abuse on the Job.* St. Louis, MO: ORCM Academic Press, 2013.

Susan Eva Porter | *Bully Nation: Why America's Approach to Childhood Aggression Is Bad for Everyone.* St. Paul, MN: Paragon House, 2013.

Walter B. Roberts | *Bullying from Both Sides: Strategic Interventions for Working with Bullies and Victims.* Thousand Oaks, CA: Corwin Press, 2006.

Rachel Simmons   *Odd Girl Out: The Hidden Culture of Aggression in Girls*. Boston: Mariner Books, 2003.

Rosalind Wiseman   *Masterminds and Wingmen: Helping Our Boys Cope with Schoolyard Power, Locker-Room Tests, Girlfriends, and the New Rules of Boy World*. New York: Harmony, 2013.

Periodicals and Internet Sources

Emily Bazelon   "Don't Be a Bystander," *Slate*, February 19, 2013. www.slate.com.

Emily Bazelon   "The Best Report on Bullying I've Ever Read," *Slate*, February 14, 2014. www.slate.com.

Christopher Bergland   "What Tactics Motivate Bullies to Stop Bullying?," *Psychology Today*, April 3, 2014.

Lenny Bernstein   "Bullying Leaves Scars Into Middle Age," *Washington Post*, April 21, 2014.

danah boyd   "'Bullying' Has Little Resonance with Teenagers," dmlcentral, November 15, 2010. www.dmlcentral.net.

danah boyd and John Palfrey   "Stop the Cycle of Bullying," *Huffington Post*, February 23, 2012. www.huffingtonpost.com.

John Cloud   "When Bullying Turns Deadly: Can It Be Stopped?," *Time*, October 24, 2010.

Lizzie Crocker "The Bully Waging War Against Bullies," Daily Beast, October 10, 2013. www.thedailybeast.com.

Randy Dotinga "Anti-Gay Bullying Tied to Teen Depression, Suicide," *U.S. News & World Report*, May 16, 2013.

Jill Filopovic "Let's Be Real: Online Harassment Isn't 'Virtual' for Women," *Talking Points Memo*, January 10, 2014. www.talkingpointsmemo.com.

Daryl Hannah "Shutting LGBT Students Out: How Current Anti-Bullying Policies Fail America's Youth," *LGBTQ Policy Journal at the Harvard Kennedy School*, 2011. www.isites.harvard.edu.

Jan Hoffman "My Coach, the Bully," *New York Times* blog, January 29, 2014. www.well.blogs.nytimes.com.

Kerry Kennedy "Changing School Culture Can End Bullying," *Washington Post*, August 11, 2013.

Marie Myung-Ok Lee "Interview with My Bully: When I Confronted My Bully About Racism," *Salon*, February 13, 2012. www.salon.com.

Raychelle Cassada Lohmann "Cyberbullying Versus Traditional Bullying," *Psychology Today*, May 14, 2012.

Amanda Marcotte "Harassment of Women Is Nothing New—The Internet Just Makes It Easier," Daily Beast, January 17, 2014. www.thedailybeast.com.

Tracy Oppenheimer "How the Anti-Bully Movement Is Hurting Kids: An Interview with Bully Nation's Susan Porter," *Reason*, April 10, 2013. www.reason.com.

Peggy Orenstein "Ending Bullying by 'Fixing' the Victims?," *New York Times* blog, November 4, 2011. www.parenting .blogs.nytimes.com.

Andrew M. Seaman "Bullying Among Kids Tied to Suicidal Thoughts, Suicide Attempts," Reuters, March 10, 2014. www .reuters.com.

Emily Thomas "Being Ignored at Work May Be Worse than Being Bullied," *Huffington Post*, June 3, 2014. www.huffingtonpost.com.

Index

A

Acceptable Use Policy (AUP), 67
Adult bullying
    beyond high school, 134–135
    dealing with, 136–137
    NFL bullying, 144–148
    police academies, 149–153
    problems in military, 154–157
    with rocks, 155–156
    school bullying of teachers,
      138–143
    types of, 135–136
    zero tolerance, 156–157
African Americans and bullying,
    114
Agatston, Patti, 84–85
Aggressive communication bully-
    ing, 135
American Fork Junior High
    School, 31
American Psychological Associa-
    tion, 76–78
Americans with Disabilities Act
    (ADA), 40
Antibullying campaigns
    masculinity and, 109–110
    overview, 107–108
    in schools, 110–112
    sexism concerns with, 107–
      112
    suicide concerns, 46
Antibullying policies, 74–75
*Archives of Pediatric and Adolescent
    Medicine* (journal), 85
Armed Services Committee, 156–
    157

Asian Americans and bullying
    local studies on, 115–116
    national data on, 114–115
    not disproportionate, 113–116
    overview, 113
    points to consider, 116
Auburn University, 125
Auld, Alison, 79–83

B

Baras, Ronit, 24
Bazelon, Emily, 19–20, 144–148
Beagley, Jessica, 23
BeatBullying charity, 38, 94–95
Berthold, Tatum, 27, 35
Bias-based bullying, 106
Bilton, Nick, 58
Bin Laden, Osama, 106
Binghamton University, 67
Bright kids as bullying targets,
    92–95
Brookshire, Jessica, 125
Bryant, Dez, 146
Buck, Nancy S., 23
*The Bully, the Bullied, and the By-
    stander* (Coloroso), 63
Bullying
    bystander effect, 34–35, 63
    decrease in, 43–44
    defined, 30–32
    emotional trauma, 38–39
    fear factor, 29–30
    focus on, 76–77
    increased reports of, 43–45
    introduction, 18–21
    lifelong problems from, 36–38

long-term effects, 32–34, 36–39

media coverage of, 47–48

overview, 23–24

panic over, 49–55

parental liability over, 40–42

suicidal thoughts, 25–27

in Utah, 25–35

See also Adult bullying; Anti-bullying campaigns; Cyber-bullying; Suicide and bullying

Bullying in college

cyberbullying, 126–129, 130–133

faculty targets, 127–129

overview, 124–125

university policies on, 129

Bullying targets

Asian Americans, 113–116

bright kids, 92–95

Hispanic and immigrants, 117–122

Muslim students, 101–106

overview, 90–91

sexism concerns, 107–112

types of bullying, 105

workplace bullying, 134–137

See also Asian Americans and bullying; police academy bulling; School bullying of teachers

Bumpus, M.F., 64

Burke, Molly, 90

Byellin, Jeremy, 40–42

Bystander effect, 34–35, 63

Byttow, David, 57

C

Calhoun School, 53

Canadian Association for Suicide Prevention, 81

Canadian Journal of Higher Education (journal), 129

CareerBuilder, 134

Carlson, Margaret, 154–157

Cartoon Network documentary, 49, 52

Cassidy, Wanda, 126–129

Castillo, Luis, 119

Castillo, Michelle, 36–39

Cellphone-based bullying, 30, 47

Center for Excellence in School Counseling and Leadership (CESCaL), 134

Centers for Disease Control and Prevention, 36, 70–71

Cheese, Aaron, 49, 55

Chen, Danny, 154–157

Child pornography, 20

Chinese Americans and bullying, 115

Cho, Margaret, 113

Christiansen, Barbara, 25–35

Clementi, Tyler, 47, 52

Clemson University, 86

Collier, Anne, 43–45

Coloroso, Barbara, 63

Columbine High School massacre, 40

Compassion fatigue, 141–142

ConnectSafely.org, 87

Controlling *vs.* teaching children, 23–24

Council on American-Islamic Relations, 101–106

Couper, David C., 149–153
Cox Communications, 85
Craig, David, 86
Craigslist, 66
Crimes Against Children Research
   Center, 44
Cross, Emma-Jane, 38
Cushing, Tim, 70–75
*Cyber Bully: Bullying in a Digital
   Age* (journal), 61
Cyber terror, 62
Cyberbullying
   anti-bullying policies, 74–75
   Asian Americans and, 113
   bystanders and, 63
   in colleges/universities, 126–
      129, 130–133
   danger of, 59–63
   defined, 59–61, 87–88
   examples, 66
   of females, 64–69
   guidelines for responding to,
      62–63
   in higher socioeconomic ar-
      eas, 31
   mental health concerns, 80–81
   no epidemic of, 85–87
   as overhyped, 70–75
   overview, 57–58, 64–65
   rates not rising, 84–85
   safety education, 71–74, 83–83
   by school kids, 34
   seriousness of, 84–88
   status and, 65–66
   strategies to address, 66–69
   traditional bullying *vs.*, 76–78
   as unreported, 61–62
   victims of, 77–78
Cyberbullying Research Center, 71,
   85–86

Cyber-Safety Act, 82
CyberTipline, 68

D

Daily Herald (newspaper), 28
Daily Mirror (newspaper), 18–19
Dalhousie University, 82
Darlington, Jeff, 147
Depression concerns, 84, 87, 98,
   105
DoSomething.org, 134
Doyle, Sady, 131
Drake, Brian, 31, 34–35
Dumas, Prin, 23
Duncan, Anne, 142
Dyer, Sarah, 94, 95

E

Education Week (journal), 43
Egnew, Michael, 146
Email bullying, 65
Emanuel, Rahm, 141, 142
*Emotional First Aid: Practical
   Strategies for Treating Failure,
   Rejection, Guilt, and Other Every-
   day Psychological Injuries*
   (Winch), 38
Emotional trauma from bullying,
   38–39
ESPN.com, 145
*European Journal of Development
   Psychology* (journal), 71

F

Facebook, 57–58, 65, 127
Facebook burn pages, 105
Faculty bullying targets, 127–129

Fader, Sarah, 19
Family Acceptance Project, 97–99
Family Matters blog, 24
Favela, Lori O., 64–69
Featherstone, Lynne, 130, 133
Fidell, Eugene, 156
Finkelhor, David, 44–45
Forbes (magazine), 124
Foundation for Individual Rights
  in Education, 52
Francis, Becky, 94
Fraser, Simon, 129

G

Galliford, Catherine, 110
García, Sergio, 118, 119, 122
Garden State Equality, 52
Gates, Bill, 142
Gelser, Sara, 90
Gender nonconforming students,
  97, 99
Gillespie, Nick, 49–55
Gillibrand, Kirsten, 156–157
Giray, Eric, 53
Goldberg, Brooke, 124
Goldstein, Steve, 52
Graff, Emma, 28
Greco, Dominic, 29
Grier, Rosey, 148

H

Hackford, Syd, 31–32
Hard Knocks (documentary), 146
Harris poll, 75
Hartford County Examiner
  (newspaper), 72–73
Hazing disadvantages, 151–153

Health implications of bullying,
  100
Healy, José A., 117–122
Higher Education Anti-
  Harassment Act, 52
Hijab wear, bullying over, 106
Hinduja, S., 64
Hispanics/immigrants and bully-
  ing
    by Latinos, 120
    at school, 121–122
    as targets, 117–118
    vulnerability of, 118–120
HIV infection concerns, 98
Holt, Rush, 52
Homophobic harassment, 61
Howard, Mahron, 28
Hubley, Jamie, 80
Hudnall, Greg, 27
Huffington Post (HuffPo), 70
Human Rights Education Center
  of Utah, 26
Humiliation bullying, 135–136

I

IMing, 65, 68
Incognito, Richie, 144–145, 147–
  148
The Independent (newspaper),
  92–95
*Indicators of School Crime and
  Safety: 2010* report, 114
International Bullying Prevention
  Association (IBPA), 85
Internet service provider (ISP), 68
Iowa State University, 85
I-Safe, 71, 73
It Gets Better campaign, 107

J

Jackson, Margaret, 129
Jenkins, Katherine, 130, 131
Jeong, Seokjin, 74
Jezebel (magazine), 19
Jones, Joshua, 32–34

K

Kalman, Izzy, 67
Kang, Cecilia, 57
Karl G. Maeser Preparatory Academy, 25, 28
Katzerman, Jerri, 118
Kennedy, Emma, 131–132
Kind Campaign, 125
Kirby, John, 156
Knight, David, 61
Korean Americans and bullying, 115

L

La Canfora, Jason, 146
Lady Gaga (pop star), 109
Latino Americans and bullying, 114, 115
Lautenberg, Frank, 52
Lesbian, gay, bisexual, and transgender (LGBT), 45, 85, 96–100, 134
Lewis, Ray, 148
Life satisfaction, 99
Limber, Susan, 86–87
Lone Peak High School, 31
Loney, Sydney, 90–91
López, Luis Carlos, 121–122
Luk, Vivian, 126–129
Lynsky, Sara, 28–29

M

Mach, Jacob, 149, 152
MacKay, Wayne, 82
Maeser Preparatory Academy, 27–28
Magid, Larry, 70, 84–88
Manipulation bullying, 136
Martin, Jonathan, 144–145, 148
Martínez, Chris, 120
Mattice, Catherine, 134–137
McBride, Kelly, 81
McChrystal, Stanley, 154
McGruff the Crime Dog, 72
Me to We organization, 91
Mean Girls (film), 65
Media coverage of bullying, 47–48
Meier, Megan, 66
Mensch, Louise, 132–133
Mental health concerns, 80–81
Military bullying, 154–157
Molloy, Parker Marie, 57
Moore, Alex, 40–41
Moore, Jill and Jim, 40, 42
Moyes, Jojo, 130–133
Muraco, J.A., 96–100
Murphy, Meghan, 107–112
Muscari, Mary, 67
Muslim students as bullying targets, 101–106
MySpace, 65

N

National Bullying Prevention Center, 90
National Center for Educational Statistics (NCES), 43, 54, 70
National Council on Disability, 90

National Crime Prevention Council (NCPC), 72, 75
National Education Association, 25
National Football League (NFL) bullies, 144–148
National Institute of Military Justice, 156
National Longitudinal Study of Adolescent Health, 114
Ne'eman, Ari, 90
Netiquette, 67
Network for Surviving Stalking, 132
The New York Times (newspaper), 58
New York Times Magazine, 149
NJ.com, 23
No Child Left Behind, 143
Non-English-speaking (NES), 122

O

Obama, Barack, 52
Office of Civil Rights, 118
Office of Safe and Drug-Free Schools, 86
Olweus, Dan, 71, 73, 75, 76–78
Olweus Bullying Questionnaire, 77
O'Neill, James, 52
Osgood, Katie, 138–143

P

Panetta, Leon, 156
Parenting concerns, 23–24, 40–42
Parsons, Rehtaeh, 80
Pascale, Lorraine, 131
Patchin, Justin, 86
Patchin, J.W., 64

Paul, Lauren, 124–125
Pediatrics (magazine), 38
Peguero, Anthony, 121
Pellegrini, Anthony, 65
Perkins, H. Wesley, 86
Perry, Jennifer, 132
Phillips, Suzanne, 59–63
Plumb, Jodi, 66
Police academy bulling
    hazing disadvantages, 151–153
    police officers *vs.* soldiers, 149–150
    problem with, 149–153
    as training, 150
Post-Traumatic Stress Disorder (PTSD), 135
Prince, Phoebe, 47, 66
Provo School District, 27
Psychological Science (magazine), 36
Psychology Today (magazine), 23

R

Rate My Professor, 128
Rehabilitation Act, 40
Rock, D., 64
Rodemeyer, Jaime, 47
Roehampton University, 93
Ross, Scott, 30–31, 34
Royal Canadian Mounted Police (RCMP), 110
Rumor spreading, 105
Russell, S.T., 96–100
Ryan, Caitlin, 97

S

Safety education, 71–74, 82–83
SafetyNETkids, 72
Sareen, Jitender, 80–81

Savage, Dan, 107
Schenecker, Julie, 23
School bullying of teachers
    compassion fatigue, 141–142
    fighting against, 142–143
    stress and abuse with, 138–140
    testing and blame, 140–141
    in workplace, 138–143
School violence declines, 44
Schwartz, Daniel J., 157
Secret for the iPhone app, 57
Sedwick, Rebecca, 59
Self-esteem concerns, 26, 98–99, 105
Sexism concerns with antibullying campaigns, 107–112
Sexual harassment, 121
Sharpe, Shannon, 148
Simon Fraser University, 126
Slate (magazine), 19
Smith, Antonio, 147
Smithhisler, Peter, 124
Social media, 45, 47
Social Psychology of Education (journal), 44
Something for the Weekend (TV show), 130
Sorority hazing, 124–125
Southern Poverty Law Center (SPLC), 118
St. Pierre, Jacques, 109
Stand for Courage Foundation, 35
Star-Ledger (newspaper), 52
Stenton, Tommy, 92–93, 95
Stopbullying.gov, 108
Suicidal thoughts, 25–27
Suicide and bullying
    adult bullying and, 135
    casual factors between, 46–48

in college, 128
cyberbullying, 59, 79, 84
ideation by LGBT young adults, 98
in military, 156
public school teachers, 138–139

T

Teen Talking Circles, 68–69
Temkin, Deborah, 46–48
Thailand, 61
Tillman, Pat, 154
TIME (magazine), 38
Todd, Amanda, 18–20
Todd, Carol, 79
Traditional bullying. *See* Bullying
Tran, Nellie, 113–116
Twitter, 57–58, 66, 131

U

United Kingdom (UK), 36
University of Bergen, 76
University of California Los Angeles, 86
University of Manitoba, 80
University of Nebraska, 147
University of New Hampshire, 44
University of Texas, 74
University of Warwick, 36
University of Washington, 68
University of Wisconsin, 124
US Department of Defense, 154
US Department of Education, 50, 86, 118
US Department of Health and Human Services, 53–54

US Department of Justice, 44,
115–116
Utah Department of Health,
25–26
Utah State University, 30

V

Verbal bullying, 105
Vietnamese Americans and bully-
ing, 116
Virginia Tech, 121

W

Wall, Tim, 81, 82–83
Wasatch Mental Health, 30
The Washington Post (newspaper),
57

Werner, N.E., 64
Wilhelm, Keiffer, 156
Willard, Nancy, 59–60
Williams, Doran, 30
Winch, Guy, 38–39
Wolke, Dieter, 36, 37
Workplace bullying, 134–137
World Mental Health Day, 82

Y

Yale University, 46
Yik Yak app, 58
Young, Jonathan, 90

Z

Zerbel, Ryan, 120
Zero tolerance, 156–157